UNITED STATES
NAVY
DIVER

Performance
Under Pressure

U.S. NAVY DIVER

Performance Under Pressure

Mark V. Lonsdale

Cover Photo Credits: Mark V. Lonsdale
                        Bev Morgan
                        Isaac Merriman

Layout Design: Jill McAdoo, Best Publishing Company
                  Rebecca Henestofel, Best Publishing Company
Editors: James T. Joiner, Best Publishing Company
                  Joel F. Russell, Best Publishing Company

International Standard Book Number: 1-930536-27-5

Library of Congress catalog card number: 2005923692

Published by:
Best Publishing Company
Post Office Box 30100
Flagstaff, AZ 86003-0100, U.S.A.

Dedication

In remembrance of SW2 (DV) Robert Stethem who lost his life to terrorists on TWA 847
14 June 1985

To the servicemen & women who lost their lives at the Pentagon, including Navy Diver Bob Dolan
11 September 2001

And to those who paid the ultimate sacrifice in Operation Enduring Freedom and Operation Iraqi Freedom
2001–On going....

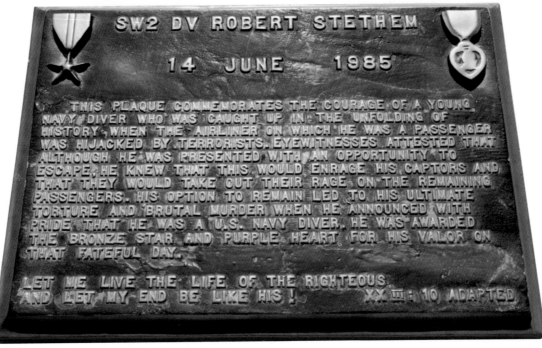

NAVY DIVER

Table of Contents

Table of Contents *(continued)*

About the Author

MARK V. LONSDALE

Mark Lonsdale is the Training Director for the Specialized Tactical Training Unit (STTU), a former deep saturation diver, and the author of several books related to diving and special operations. His responsibilities at STTU encompass most aspects of law enforcement and military special operations training, including program development and training of dive teams, primarily in the areas of search & recovery, dignitary protection, narcotics interdiction, and maritime operations.

In addition, for the past fourteen years Mark has served as a diver, diving supervisor, and Training Officer for the Los Angeles Sheriff's Special Enforcement Bureau Marine Company Dive Team, and the reserve component of the Emergency Services Detail. He is also a member of the Sheriff's Diving Control Board, a co-author of the Sheriff's Diving Guidelines, and has received numerous letters of commendation for hazardous operations, including the recovery of three victims from flooded mines in 2001, and another three from 260 feet in a deep mountain lake following a fatal boat accident.

Mark has assisted the US military with other hazardous operations, both diving and non-diving, and donated his time as a lecturer and Diving Instructor-Trainer in the UCLA Underwater Kinesiology Program under renowned diving physiologist Dr Glen Egstrom.

Before entering the military, Mark was a member of the national judo team and had worked as a civil marine construction diver, and then after as a deep saturation diver in the North Sea where he racked up several thousand hours at depths down to 500 fsw.

Since the tragic events of 9-11, Mark has been actively involved in the training of US military and coalition special forces for deployment in support of Operations Enduring Freedom and Iraqi Freedom. The L.A. Sheriff's dive team has also been involved in homeland security focused on shipping and port facility security and underwater search operations.

Acknowledgements

Thinking back to my days as a young student at deep sea diving school, where the US Navy Diving Manual was our "bible," I could not have imagined the day when I would not only come to meet the US Navy Supervisor of Diving but would actually come to call him a friend. I have also come to know many other fine men and women in the US Navy diving community whose support has made this book possible. My sincere thanks go out to all of them.

This *Navy Diver* began with a call to the Los Angeles PAO, CDR Bob Anderson, who passed me to the folks at CHINFO: Commander Graham, LCDR Skelton, and LT David Blackwood—who in turn green-lighted the project.

Individuals who made a unique and valuable contribution include: Captain Mark "Kamper" Helmkamp, Supervisor of Diving and former CO of the NDSTC; CDR Barbara "Bobbie" Scholley, former SUPDIVE and CO of MDSU2; Mike Ward, former NEDU and deep saturation diver; and Connie-Lynn Morgan and Bev Morgan of Kirby-Morgan.

Several of the images of this book came from Naval Visual Services so thanks go to:

Christopher J. Madden, Director Navy Visual News; LCDR Paul Jensen, Deputy Director; Mrs. Henrietta Wright, and LT Rick Naystatt. Additional images also came from the very professional divers and photographers of Fleet Combat Camera: PHC (SW/DV) Andy McKaskle, Navy Diver Lippman, and PH2(SW/DV) Isaac Merriman.

At NDSTC: CDR Jon D. Kurtz, Debbie Cropper, LCDR Jim Bredemeier, Training Officer LCDR Dave Randall, Command Master Chief MMCM (MDV) Schnoering, Jack "JR" Hott in the Helmet Locker, LT Carolyn Wisner, and CWO4 Terry Harris.

At NEDU, CDR Erik Christensen, XO LCDR Sanders, Command Master Chief MDV Don Curtis, LCDR Timothy Libertore, and Bob Barth, and at CSS, Rob Cole in audio-visual services, Barry Miller, Bill Gavin, and base PAO Steve Applegate.

I was welcomed aboard at CDU by Commander Richard Kelly Eley and CWO4 Armstrong, and on the *USS Constellation* project by Command Master Chief (MDV) "Brick" Bradford, HTC (MDV) Chief Bob Barker, BM1 (DV) Dave Sator, BM2 (DV) Michael Wiltshire, and Second Class Divers HT2 Tyson Hoover and HT2 Dave Real.

At COMSUBPAC, PAO LT Christy Sheaff, CDU DET MDV Boy Kayona.

I owe special thanks to the command at MDSU-1 for hosting me during the very sensitive *Ehime Maru* diving operations: CO Commander Robert Fink, XO LCDR Ron "Leith" Parslow, OPS Officer LCDR George Byford, EM diving coordinator CWO3 George Primavera, Command Master Chief MMCM (DSW/MDV) Jim Nichols, HTCS (DSW/MDV) Bill Cridis, BMC (MDV/DSWS/SW/AW) Doug Westling, and from the *USS Salvor*, BMCS(MDV) Orns.

At MDSU-2 and on the *Monitor* project, CDR Barbara "Bobbie" Scholley, SUPDIVE CAPT Chris Murray, CWO3 Master Diver Frank Perna, CDR Bill Robertson, LCDR Geof McCauley, Ed Eidson, LT Doug Smith, DMO LT Julianna Lippert, LT Paul Ware, MDV Mallet, IS3 Sutherland, HT2 Duncan, Chief Landon St. Peter, Carol Meyers with NOAA, CWO3 Dave Thompson, DV Neil Patterson, and CAPT Chip McCord for use of his article on the TWA incident.

At SIMA, CW02 Mikulski, MDV Douglas Roberson, and PAO Chief David Johnson; and at UCT, LCDR Greg Zielinski, LCDR Brant Pickrell, Brett Blanton, and PAO Daryl Smith.

At EOD GROUP ONE, CAPT Michael Tillotson, CAPT William Wright, CDR Jeff Trumbore, PAO LT Terrisiana Lee, LT Jean Carrillo, Chief Jaculin Peterson, LCDR Bob Baughman, LCDR Clark Nichols, CDR Adam Guziewicz, LCDR Michael "Mickey" Pierce, CWO Ted Dingle, LT John Drennen, Warrant Officer Darcy. At EODMU3, MDV Rood, MM2(DV)Brent Wadsworth, AO1 Mark Harrison; at EODMU7, LCDR Randy Packard, LT Kent

Keller, LT Kevin Staples, and LT Bryon Kibildis; and at NSCT1, CDR Tony Rogers, LCDR Jay Richards, CMC Kurt Nelson, LT Paul Barrie, and QM1 (SWCC/DV/PJ) Scott Keough. At SPECWARCOM, CAPT Bill McCraven, LCDR Darryn James, LCDR Jeff Alderson, LT Katie Licup, Trish O'Conner, LT Tamsen McCabe, Ensign B. Mann.

At NSWG2, LCDR Denise Shorey; at SDVT1, CWO2 Rick Strynar, BMCS(MDV) Pascal Balesi and Pete McDermott; and at SDVT2, CMDR Roger Herbert, Master Chief Bryan Bracket, HMCS Gaetano Giuliano, and CWO2 Peter Sharpe.

USMC PAOs Captain Matt Morgan and Capt Shawn Hayes, who passed me to Captain Wes Hayes, LT Ward, LT Bennett, and Staff Sergeant Jamison at Camp Pendleton Marine Corps Base. At the Recon Amphibious Dive Locker, I was in the good hands of Master Diver Mark Leet, Gunny Karl Foisy, EN1 (SW/DV) Smith, and master rigger SSgt Matt Johnson. Access to the 1st Force Recon training operations was granted by LTC Boyle and Major Anthony Herlihy, and I was privileged to work with 5th Platoon's Captain Steve Fiscus, Gunny Blakey, and Recon Marine Carey Wells.

For the fine line artwork, William Abell, Richard M. Fitzpatrick, "Black Bart" Bartholomew, and the US Navy Diving Manual.

For historical material, Leslie Leany with the Historical Diving Society, Joe Fontana Jr., MVD Ramos, Charlie Orr with CCED, Ken Downey at Morse, John Gallagan aka Captain John, Jim Boyd, Steven Waterman, and Patrick Stethem.

Last but not least, to all the nameless US Navy personnel who composed text for the myriad of official Navy diving-related websites. Their efforts saved me weeks of research for this project, and in some cases I have "borrowed" whole blocks of text with only minor re-editing.

Note: In doing historical research, one frequently finds discrepancies in names, dates, and places, for after all, history is often derived from the scrawled notes and recollections of some yeoman or secretary, written some time after the fact. If the reader should find errors in this book, please contact the author directly so these can be adjusted in future editions—Email: MVLonsdale@aol.com

Foreword

This book presents an exciting pictorial of the US Navy diver's techniques and equipment, from the evolution of US Navy diving to the intensive training of dive teams. Whether you are in the US Navy or just a proud American, you will find this book useful and informative. The photographs illustrate the developmental history of US Navy divers, from ancient brass helmets to real-life divers in action and brought back fond memories of my own experiences diving the venerable MK V Deep-Sea rig.

Mark V. Lonsdale has succeeded in reviewing the technology and exhilaration of US Navy diving in a comprehensive manner. I am certain anyone who reads this book will share in the experiences it depicts and will learn from Mark's enhanced knowledge of the US Navy. Readers will absorb the text and photographs with a feeling of pride and appreciation for those who have served our nation as Navy Divers.

Captain Mark Helmkamp, United States Navy
Supervisor of Diving

Introduction

There is a deep personal pride of almost mythic proportion associated with being a "deep-sea diver." This is reflected in the history and traditions of the diving community and graphically illustrated on dive team t-shirts depicting brawny hard-hat divers, watched over by King Neptune and adored by voluptuous mermaids. The tattoos and bar-room stories only add to the legend and folklore. However, this deep rooted pride is hard to explain to those who do not possess a passion for diving or share the diver's desire to take on dangerous tasks that more timid souls would shy away from.

Not unlike the astronaut in space, the deep-sea diver works in a hostile environment and is totally dependent on artificial life support—far below the surface of the ocean where a reliable supply of breathable air or mixed-gas is a necessity. A place where seemingly minor mistakes can have terminal consequences.

The diver must overcome man's natural aversion for deep, dark water and contend with not only bone-chilling cold and strong currents, but also the myriad of dangers that go with working under pressure. Gas mixtures that are harmless on the surface can become toxic under pressure; nitrogen narcosis can cloud the mind, leaving a diver helpless at depth; the insidious bends, decompression sickness, painful in mild cases, can leave a diver crippled for life in more severe cases. Even the air that is so essential to life on this planet will kill the diver at extreme depth.

If these were not enough, the diver must contend with the inherent dangers of working salvage and heavy construction underwater—trapped in unstable wreckage, cut by razor sharp metal, blown up by explosive gas pockets, sucked into active intake pipes, crushed by cranes, or run over by boats. All for what—the glory? Not hardly.

With deep-sea diving there is not even the satisfaction that a firefighter or police officer may derive from making the six o'clock news—their heroic deeds caught on tape to be seen by millions of viewers. The diver works alone in cold, dark silence disturbed only by the sound of his own breathing and the bubbles from his helmet. He is judged solely on the results of his endeavor and seeks only the acceptance and respect of his peers.

So what is it that makes an individual choose such a physically demanding job so fraught with danger? For those city dwellers doomed to an existence in high-rise offices, congested cities, and dirty factories, there would be the allure of not having to deal with traffic, of working in the ocean realm, and of breathing not only clean but purified air. For those trying to escape mind-numbing, repetitive jobs, there would be the international travel and the excitement of not knowing what or where the next job may be. San Diego or Norfolk today, the Persian Gulf or South Pacific tomorrow.

The deep-sea diver is a different animal, coming to diving not out of frustration of a benign existence but the need to be someone special and live the dream—a dream that would be a nightmare for the weak of heart or body.

Ask any gray-haired deep-sea diver (the author included) and he will tell you how he was influenced by the 1957 *Sea Hunt* television series starring Lloyd Bridges as the intrepid Mike Nelson, or the early documentaries made by Cousteau and his lead diver Albert Falco. In Master Diver Karneke's memoirs from the late 1930s, he talks about being influenced by "Jake," the silent sentinel in full MK V diving dress at the Naval Training Station, Newport, RI, where he was a new recruit attending gunnery school.

But what of the new divers arriving at the Navy Dive School today—influenced not by television from the sixties but high tech entertainment and space travel of the new millennium. For one young Navy Diver, it was nothing more than a 30-second news clip on television. Back in April of 2001, while working on this book, I was privileged to dive with the

Navy's Consolidated Divers Unit (CDU), documenting their efforts to repair the rudder on the aircraft carrier *USS Constellation*. This was a high priority job and the pressure was on, since the fleet, including some 20,000 sailors and Marines, was waiting to put to sea.

The problem was a large keyway cross-pin that secured the rudder to the rudder shaft had broken inside the rudder and the CDU divers were working to get the broken pieces out, to be replaced with a new key. It was one of those nasty jobs that frustrated the dive team as they jumped diver after diver and employed different techniques to first access the massive steel wedge and then remove it.

By the time I arrived on site they had burned an access hole in the side of the rudder and were drilling into one end with a heavy-duty underwater drill to try and budge the stubborn block of steel. I immediately suited up, jumped in and followed the diver's umbilical down through a maze of rigging, hydraulic hoist hoses, air lines, and welding cables to where he was working.

While shooting photos of the diver drilling into the heavy pin, deep under the carrier and in poor visibility, the Navy diver felt the key move and began the painstaking process of maneuvering it out, careful not to crush his fingers.

Thirty minutes later, after a tricky lift-bag operation, both pieces of the broken key lay on the deck as the tender removed the MK 21 hat from what I now saw to be a very young "Two Charlie" (Navy Diver Second Class). The look on the faces of the NAVSEA engineers and CDU dive supervisor showed both pleasure and relief, knowing that they were over the hump and could now begin the easier but more technical task of installing the new key and aligning the rudder. They had 24 hours to get the fleet to sea.

For the next hour there was a stream of senior officers from the carrier coming down to the work barge to see the broken key and congratulate the young Navy diver. Seemingly unimpressed by all the outside attention, the diver was nevertheless pleased with the fact that he had made the CDU divers look good and earned the respect of his Dive Sup and teammates in the process.

Later that day, as he was taking his turn in the rotation as stand-by diver, I took the time to find out more about his Navy dive training—my first question being, "What got you interested in being a Navy diver?"

Instead of the expected answer, HT2 Hoover said, "Back when I was in high school, I saw some Navy divers working on an aircraft crash on the news. I thought that looked like a cool job, so I decided to join the Navy."

TWA Flight 800, a Paris-bound Boeing 747, exploded and crashed off Long Island, NY, shortly after leaving JFK Airport, killing all 230 souls aboard. Eyewitnesses reported two explosions and a fire on the surface of the ocean. Fueled by the media, theories abounded on why this aircraft exploded and crashed.

Naval salvage assets were brought to bear and a total of 226 Navy divers from 23 different commands logged over 4,344 dives. But this heroic effort was lost to the viewing public. Most people were drawn to the tragedy of the crash, the victims and their families, but for at least one young viewer, it was all about the tough-looking characters in the yellow and chrome helmets descending into the depths of the Atlantic.

That was July 1996 and less than five years later, this same young man was not only a sailor and Hull Technician in the most powerful Navy in the world, he was also a Navy deep-sea diver being congratulated by Senior Chiefs, Commanders, and Captains for a difficult job well done.

With the ever increasing demand for US Navy divers the world over, hopefully young men and women will continue to be drawn by the challenge and traditions of deep-sea diving. For anyone seeking inspiration, they need only read *The Terrible Hours,* in which author Peter Maas recounts the 1939 heroics of Lieutenant Commander "Swede" Momsen and his divers. This group of Navy deep-sea diving pioneers first rescued the survivors of the *USS Squalus,* sunk in 243 feet of water off the eastern seaboard; they then salvaged the submarine to be repaired and returned to the fleet. The rescue divers were awarded the Congressional Medal of Honor, the only CMHs awarded to any servicemen between the two World Wars.

Evolution of U.S. Navy Diving

Although *NAVY DIVER* primarily documents US Navy diving today, it is important to appreciate the significant influence that US Navy research and development has had on all aspects of military and commercial diving. Driven by the need to have deep submarine rescue, salvage capabilities, and other more classified projects, the divers, scientists, and engineers of the US Navy diving program have spent over a century pushing the limits of human endurance and technology to improve both diver safety and operational capabilities.

As far back as the eighteen hundreds, but more in the early nineteen hundreds, the US Navy was involved in deep salvage operations and had already gained an appreciation for the limits of deep air diving and the need for better equipment and techniques.

However, in reading the following time-line, keep in mind that it was young, and some not-so-young, Navy divers who volunteered to make the hazardous dives required in developing the decompression tables and diving equipment in use today. Even with the benefits afforded by science and technology in the form of remote operated vehicles (ROV), there inevitably comes the time when a diver must make the plunge, helmet secured to his head and tools in hand, to perform the difficult tasks that modern machines still cannot.

Augustus Siebe's first design of an open diving helmet. Circa 1829.

HIGHLIGHTS OF DIVING HISTORY (1828 – 2004)

Though most of the following dates relate to US Navy diving, it would be remiss to omit the contributions of early British inventors such as Augustus Siebe and Sir Robert Davis, eminent Scottish physiologist John Scott Haldane, the Royal Navy, and a particular French Naval Lieutenant.

Many of these dates have been drawn from early editions of the US Navy Diving Manual, some of which had errors that hopefully have been corrected here, while others were researched from a variety of diving-related books and historical papers.

Augustus Siebe's first design of a closed diving helmet, having three view ports, 12 bolt breastplate, and spitcock. The relieved screw joint connecting both the top and bottom parts of the helmet is non-recessed.

1828 Englishmen Charles & John Deane, based on earlier work in 1823 developing a "smoke helmet," devise a similar helmet with a diving suit. However, the suit was not attached to the helmet, so a diver could not bend over or invert without risk of flooding the helmet and drowning. Nevertheless, the diving system was used in salvage work, including the successful removal of cannon from the British warship HMS *Royal George* in 1834 & 1835. This 108-gun fighting ship had sunk in 65 feet of water at Spithead anchorage in 1783.

1837 Morse & Fletcher Brass Goods is established in Boston, Massachusetts. Morse would go on to become a significant manufacturer of diving helmets.

1839 Combining advancements in diving dress design, Augustus Siebe manufactures his first Siebe Closed Dress combination helmet and suit. By bolting the helmet to the suit, this closed system enabled the diver to assume various positions underwater, such as inverting, that the Deane's open helmet could not. This was to be the foundation on which diving dresses of the future were based (Siebe Gorman, the company founded by Siebe, went on to manufacture helmets continuously until 1975).

Siebe's closed dress.

1840 The British Navy orders the Siebe Closed Dress for work on the recovery of cannon from the *Royal George* and subsequent blasting to clear the anchorage. The Admiralty hails the Siebe diving equipment as a significant improvement in diving equipment for the time. Subsequently, the "Siebe Improved Diving Dress" is adopted as the standard diving dress by the Royal Engineers. It was during the *Royal George* recovery work that Siebe introduced the interrupted-thread neckring to the diving helmet, allowing the helmet to be detached from the breastplate and completing the modern design.

1843 Based on lessons learned from the *Royal George* salvage, the first diving school is set up by the Royal Navy.

1844 Augustus Schrader's diving equipment company is founded in Brooklyn, New York, later to become A. Schrader's Son, Inc.

1864 Morse company name changes to Andrew J. Morse & Son.

1869 US Naval Torpedo Station is established in Newport, Rhode Island, and soon needs divers for torpedo recovery. This resulted in the establishment of the Navy's first dive school in 1882 at the Newport Torpedo Station.

1876 English merchant seaman Henry Fleuss develops the first workable, self-contained diving rig that uses compressed oxygen. This prototype of closed-circuit scuba utilized rope soaked in caustic potash to absorb carbon dioxide so that the exhaled gas can be re-breathed.

1882 The US Navy's first diving school is established at the Newport Torpedo Station, Rhode Island.

1905 Several sources, including the 1991 US Navy Dive Manual (pp 1–18), state that the MK V Deep Sea Diving Dress was designed by the Bureau of Construction & Repair in 1905, but in reality, the 1905 Navy Handbook shows British Siebe-Gorman helmets in use. Since the earliest known MK V is dated 1916, these sources are probably referring to the earlier MK I & MK II Morse helmets, and the MK III & MK IV helmets made by Schrader.

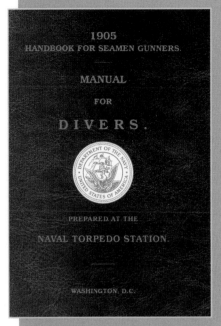

U.S. Navy Diving Manual 1905.

A.J. Morse & Son, of Boston, had been manufacturing diving equipment since 1837. In the early 1930s, Morse designed the shallow-water helmet with a large, curved, shatter-proof glass window.

The final lift of the submarine F-4 was made using these submarine salvage pontoons designed by Naval Constructor Julius A. Furer. Raised—N.Y. Harbor, Long Island Sound.

1908 John Scott Haldane, Arthur E. Boycott, and Guybon C. Damant publish their landmark paper on decompression sickness, "The Prevention of Compressed-Air Illness," which laid the foundation for staged decompression. Decompression tables based on this research were eventually adopted by the British Navy and later the United States Navy, saving many divers from the bends.

1912 US Navy Chief Gunner George Stillson sets up a program to test diving tables and staged decompression theory based on the work of Haldane.

1913 The US Navy also begins design improvements to the future MK V, influenced by Schrader and Morse designs.

1915 The submarine USS *F-4* is salvaged from 304 feet, establishing the practical limits for air diving. Three U.S. Navy divers, Chief Crilley, Loughman, and Ensign Nielson, reached 304 fsw using current US Navy equipment (possibly an early version of the MK V).

1916 With the addition of a battery-powered telephone, the design of the MK V is finalized —however, several more design improvements were made over the next two years.

Based on lessons learned from the *F-4* salvage, the Navy Dive School is established at Newport, Rhode Island.

1917 The Bureau of Construction & Repair introduces the MK V helmet and dress, which then becomes the standard for US Navy diving until the introduction of the MK 12 in 1980.

1918 End of World War I.

1924 The US Navy and Bureau of Mines jointly sponsor experimental dives using helium-oxygen mixtures.

One of the first versions of the Mark V helmet.

1925 With the sinking and subsequent salvage of the submarine *S-51*, the Navy discovers that they had only 20 divers qualified to dive deeper than 90 feet—a result of post-World War I cutbacks.

1927 Driven by a need for divers, the Navy School of Diving & Salvage (NSDS) is reestablished at the Washington Navy Yard. To bring diving assets together, the Experimental Diving Unit (EDU) was also brought in from Pittsburgh where they had been working with the Bureau of Mines.

The weight of the MK V helmet and breastplate was reduced to 56 pounds with little change in the design thereafter.

*Charles "Swede" Bowers Momsen.
A pioneer of submarine rescue
and deep mixed-gas diving.*

1928 Invention of the Davis Submersible Decompression Chamber (SDC) diving bell.

1929 Lieutenant C.B. "Swede" Momsen, a submariner and diver, develops and proves the escape lung that bears his name. It was given its first operational test when 26 officers and men successfully surfaced from an intentionally bottomed submarine.

1936 The Italian Navy tests a diver-controlled chariot torpedo system.

1937 Lieutenant Commander Momsen heads up the experimental deep-sea diving unit at the Washington Navy Yard. NEDU presses a diver to 500 feet on helium mixed-gas.

Diving Equipment & Salvage Company, now known as DESCO, is organized as a corporation in Wisconsin by divers Max Nohl & Jack Browne, along with doctor and hyperbaric physiologist Edgar End, MD.

December—Max Nohl succeeds in diving to a depth of 420 feet in the cold waters of Lake Michigan, thereby breaking a depth record held by U.S. Navy diver Frank Crilley since 1915. Nohl accomplished this feat using DESCO's new diving equipment and breathing a heli-ox mixture prescribed by Dr. Edgar End.

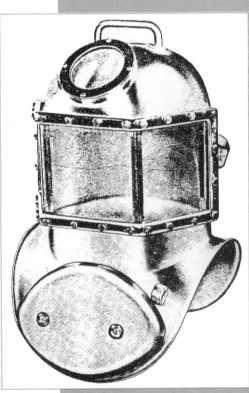

1938 Dr. Edgar End and Max Nohl make the first intentional saturation dive, spending 27 hours at a depth of 101 feet in a Milwaukee hospital hyperbaric chamber. Decompression took five hours and one of the divers, Nohl, suffered the bends.

*DESCO, founded in 1937 as the
Diving Equipment and Salvage
Company, produced a shallow-
water helmet in the early 1940s
that had three flat windows plus
a top port for maximum
visibility.*

The type of helmet used in fully dressed diver shown below.

1939 The McCann-Erickson Rescue Chamber, actually developed by Momsen, is proven when the USS *Squalus*, carrying a crew of 59, sinks in 243 fsw. Under the direction of Lieutenant Commander "Swede" Momsen, the rescue chamber made four trips and safely brought 33 men to the surface.

Momsen's divers, using both air and mixed-gas diving techniques, recover the USS *Squalus* from 243 fsw. Based on this success, the Navy soon adopted a re-circulating MK V MOD 1 for mixed-gas diving. Helmet and breastplate weighed 103 pounds, as opposed to the 56 pounds for the standard MK V air hat.

1940 Owen Churchill first produces swim fins. Initially less than a thousand pairs are sold, but in later years production increases substantially as thousands were sold to Allied forces during WWII.

1941 (WWII). Italian naval divers, working out of midget submarines, make use of closed-circuit scuba to place explosives under British naval and merchant ships. Later in the war the British use this technology to attempt to sink the German battleship *Tirpitz*.

U.S. Navy develops its first mine disposal school after examining the German mine problems confronted by Great Britain.

December 7, 1941. The Imperial Japanese forces bomb Pearl Harbor.

1942 September—In addition to NSDS at Washington Navy Yard, the Naval Training School (Salvage) is established in New York. This was to take advantage of the training value in salvaging the *Normandie*, capsized at New York City's Pier 88 as a result of fire-fighting efforts.

In the Pearl Harbor salvage operations, Navy divers spend an estimated 16,000 hours under water performing some 4,000 dives. Contract civilian divers contributed another 4,000 diving hours to the effort.

In addition to Schrader and Morse, DESCO begins manufacturing the MK V for the US Navy and by 1945 was reported to be the largest diving equipment manufacturer in the world.

French Navy Lieutenant Jacques-Yves Cousteau and Emile Gagnan, an engineer for Air Liquide, redesign a car regulator that will automatically provide compressed air to a diver on demand.

1943 Bomb disposal experts and Navy Seabees (Construction Battalion) team up to develop techniques to remove obstacles from enemy waters. Naval Combat Demolition Units (NCDU), predecessors of the UDTs, are formed and serve with distinction in the Pacific and at Normandy in 1944.

Cousteau, Frederic Dumas, and Philippe Tailliez make over 500 dives with the Aqua Lung, gradually increasing the depths on each dive. This is the first workable, open-circuit, demand-type scuba regulator. In October Dumas reaches 210 feet in the Mediterranean Sea.

1945 End of World War II.

1946 Under new ownership, Desco changes its name to Diving Equipment & Supply Company, Inc.

Civilian diver Jack Browne, shareholder in Desco and inventor of the lightweight full-face mask that bears his name, makes a simulated dive to 550 feet in Desco's pressurized wet pot.

Naval Training School (Salvage) moved from New York to Bayonne, New Jersey.

The British Admiralty Experimental Diving Unit was established.

1947 Establishment of the combined, all-service Naval School Explosive Ordnance Disposal (NAVSCOLEOD). Later moved to Indian Head, Maryland.

Using Cousteau's Aqua Lung, Frederic Dumas makes a record dive to 307 feet in the Mediterranean.

LCDR Doug Fane makes advances in UDT diving and submarine operations.

Robert B. Sheats stands beside an exact duplicate of a Morse shallow water hat, with a depth limit of 90 feet, which he was forced to use when working to recover Phillippine pesos as a Japanese prisoner.

Chest weight.

Diver ready to descend.

*Air diver shoes —
made of leather,
lead-plate soles, and
brass toe-caps,
approximate weight
21 lbs. each.*

*An early style
weight belt.*

*The U.S. Navy training tank at
New London, Connecticut. The
130-foot tank is used for diving
experiments and submarine
escape training.*

*An early hard hat
diver standing next
to his "air pump."*

Navy Diving Crew in mid-1940s
Standing (left to right): Russ Johnson,
Joe Amaro, Bill Biller, Jack Shay.
Divers: Buck Scougal and Ed Goodrich.

An early standard Navy dive boat.

1948 A British Navy diver sets an open-sea record of 540 feet.

1949 The Aqua-Lung SCUBA system is adopted for UDT operations.

1950 Underwater Demolition Teams (UDT) see action in the Korean conflict.

1951 A. Schrader produces their last helmets.

1952 Development of the US Navy Emerson-Lambertsen closed-circuit oxygen rebreather. LCDR Fane dives to 252 feet to destroy classified equipment on a crashed USAF bomber.

MK V mixed-gas helmet.

MK V mixed-gas helmet.

MK V helmet.

These two photos show the Mark III Morse diving pump. Note the two holes near the edge of wheel on each side of pump. A handle or pipe was inserted to be used for turning the wheels.

1954 Development of the prototype Mark VI semi-closed circuit mixed-gas rebreather for explosive ordnance disposal (introduced in 1963).

1955 "Swede" Momsen retires from the Navy with the rank of Vice Admiral.

1956 NEDU publishes the USN Standard Decompression Tables.

A Royal Navy diver reaches 600 feet in open sea on a helium-oxygen mix.

1957 The first episode of SEA HUNT airs, and has a strong influence on many future deep-sea divers, the author included.

Genesis Project experiments conducted as the pre-cursor of Navy saturation diving.

1958 USS *Nautilus* successfully passes under the North Pole.

1960 January 23, Jacques Picard and Navy Lt. Don Walsh, in the US Navy-owned, Swiss-built bathyscaphe *Trieste*, descend to 35,820 fsw (10,916 msw, 6.78 miles). The dive is made in the Pacific's Mariana Trench, 250 miles southwest of Guam.

Auxilary submarine rescue vessel
USS Sunbird *entering Valleta*
Harbor in Malta, 1961.

*Crew aboard #5 dive boat
Torpedo Range at Newport,
Rhode Island.
Note: In background, US Navy
first chamber (Rivet).*

*Chief Petty Officer, Al
Nesbitt, receiving a
Honorable Discharge
required to get his
shipping order to the
USS Fulton.*

*Hard hat diver in training—
going through the task of putting
together the "pipe puzzle."*

Bayonne, NJ, Class #56, 1954.

1962 US Navy SEAL Teams 1 and 2 are formed.

With partial support of the US Navy, Swiss diver Hannes Keller reaches over 1,000 feet off California.

September — First practical saturation dive. Edward A. Link's program has one man breathing helium-oxygen at 200 fsw for 24 hours in a specially designed diving system.

1963 April—USS *Thresher* sinks in 8,400 feet of water, beyond crush and recovery depths.

1964 Formation of the Deep Submergence Systems Project (DSSP).

Sealab 1, under the direction of Captain George F. Bond, places four men underwater for 11 days at an average depth of 193 fsw.

Navy adopts the MK 6 UBA semi-closed circuit rebreather for combat swimmers and EOD (maximum depth 200 fsw).

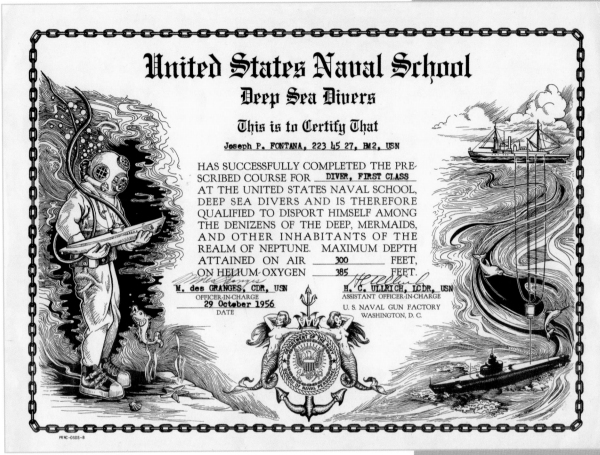

U.S. Navy diver Joe Fontana.

Joe Fontana, front row, hand on helmet. Carl Brashear, standing second from right (1954).

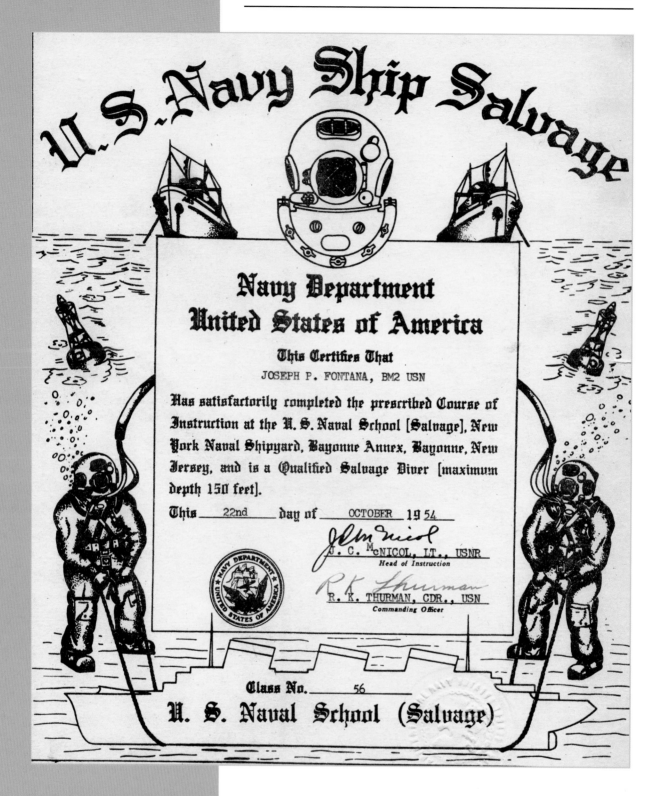

1965 Bob Kirby and Bev Morgan form Kirby-Morgan.

Sealab II puts three teams of ten men each in a habitat on the coast of California. Each team spends 15 days at depth and one man, Astronaut Scott Carpenter, remains for 30 days.

1966 Harbor Clearance Unit ONE (HCU-1) commissioned.

DESCO is purchased by new owners and moved to current location in Milwaukee.

1967 May 25—"Swede" Momsen loses his battle with cancer and is missed by all. NDSTC would later be named in his honor.

The first DDS & SDS-450 Deep Diving System was placed in Fleet Service by Harbor Clearance Unit ONE.

Kirby-Morgan manufactures the KMB-8 Bandmask.

SEAL Teams 1 & 2 deploy in Vietnam.

1968 A record-breaking excursion dive to 1,025 feet is made from a saturation depth of 825 feet at NEDU.

The MK-2 Mod 0 Deep Diving System is developed and put aboard the *Elk River* (IX-501) to support Sealab III.

1969 February—Sealab III ends in disaster with the death of diver Berry Cannon at over 600 fsw. He had been given a MK IX diving rig with no CO_2 absorbent.

1970 The DDS MK-1 Deep Diving System comes into service. In October a world record open-sea dive is made to 850 feet.

Diving officer speaks on telephone with divers at bottom.

Coming up from a dive, the diver grasps the stage bails and is swung aboard by the tenders. (On standard deep sea dress, legs are laced to prevent them from inflating and ballooning the diver upside down to the surface.)

Circa 1978. Diver on the Polaris missile test platforms at 210 feet.

1971 Saturation divers, deploying from submarines, have considerable success in Cold War intelligence collection missions.

1972 The DDS MK-2 MOD 0 sets the in-water record of 1,010 fsw.

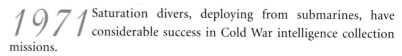

First Deep Submergence Rescue Vehicle (DSRV) becomes operational.

1973 ASR-21 *Pigeon* & ASR-22 *Ortolan* are commissioned and equipped as DSRV, submarine rescue, and saturation diving support platforms.

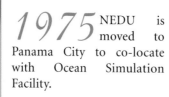

Aquanaut Berry Cannon.

1975 NEDU is moved to Panama City to co-locate with Ocean Simulation Facility.

Divers using the MK 1 Deep Dive System descend to 1,148 fsw.

MDV Brick Bradford at Second Class Dive School.

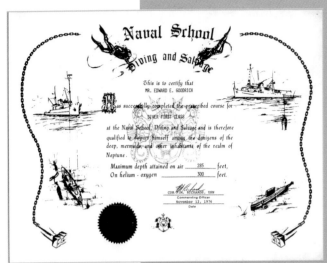

1976 Based on the Kirby-Morgan KMB-10 Bandmask, the U.S. Navy approves the MK-1 MOD 0 Light-weight, Mixed-Gas Diving Outfit for dives to 300 fsw on helium-oxygen. The Kirby-Morgan SuperLite-17B goes into production and the KMB-10 is upgraded as the DSI Heli-Ox 18.

1977 The MK 1 Deep Diving System goes out of service.

The author makes the first of many deep saturation dives in the North Sea, benefiting from the tables developed by NEDU.

A French dive team breaks the open-sea record with a dive to 1,643 fsw.

1978 NEDU develops the Mark 11 semi-closed system and the Mark 14 "push/pull system" for use in conjunction with an umbilical to a personnel transfer capsule (PTC), more commonly called a diving bell, to extend saturation dive times.

1979 The MK 15 mixed-gas closed-circuit rebreather replaces the MK 6 UBA.

Divers from NEDU complete a 37-day, 1,800 fsw dive in its Ocean Simulation Facility (OSF).

1980 The new Naval Diving & Salvage Training Center (NDSTC) is completed on the Coastal Systems Station reservation in Panama City, Florida.

After extensive development, the MK 12 Surface-Supplied Diving System (SSDS) replaces the MK V MOD 1 mixed-gas heavy gear.

1981 A record 2,250-foot dive is made in the Duke Medical Center chamber.

The deepest salvage operation, with divers at 803 fsw, is made when divers retrieved 431 gold ingots from the wreck of HMS *Edinburgh*, sunk during the war between Germany and Russia.

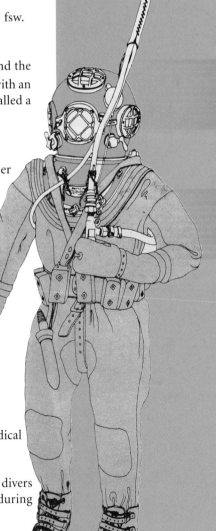

*The exterior of the "Iron Doctor,"
the diver's recompression tank.*

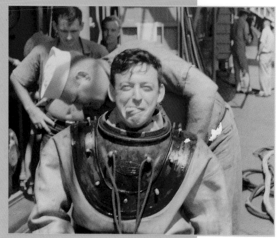

*MC BM MDV Juan Ramos.
Ramos made a 365' gas dive in
the Gulf of Tonkin, South East
Asia, in 1968/1969, and a 945'
sat dive at San Clemente Island
in 1972/73.*

USN MK12 SSDS helmet.

1982 The Draeger LAR V (MK-25) closed-circuit oxygen rebreather replaces the MK 6 Emerson-Lambertsen rebreather for shallow water combat swimmers.

The first Dry Deck Shelter (DDS) for Swimmer Delivery Vehicles (SDVs) is completed by the Electric Boat Division of General Dynamics Corporation.

1983 Navy SEALs deployed in Grenada, Operation Urgent Fury.

1985 The MK 12 is officially approved for Fleet use to replace the MK V heavy gear.

New low-magnetic MK 16 approved for EOD.

1988 An open-sea dive is made to 1,650 fsw.

1989 Navy SEALs and EOD divers deployed in Panama, Operation Just Cause.

1990 The MK-1 MOD 0 bandmask is replaced by the MK 21 MOD 1 demand helmet.

Navy SEALs and EOD divers deployed in "Operation Desert Storm."

1993 December—The MK 21 Superlite-style diving helmet replaces the MK 12.

1994 Driven by the high cost of helium, in a joint effort, Kirby-Morgan and Divex develop the Divex UltraJewel 601 gas reclaim system.

1997 Navy diving and salvage assets are used in the recovery of TWA 800.

1999 MDSU2 recovers the screw of the Civil War ironclad *Monitor.*

Navy begins test and evaluation of the Advanced SEAL Delivery System (ASDS) off Hawaii.

EOD and MDSU divers respond to Aden in support of the USS *Cole* after the attack by terrorists.

2001 SEALs authorized to begin using the new NAVY Dive Computer built by Cochran.

The Navy utilizes a saturation diving system for use on the *Monitor* project and recovers the engine.

US Navy SUPSALV recovers the Japanese fishing vessel *Ehime Maru* from 2,000 feet of water off Hawaii after being accidentally sunk by the *USS Greeneville.* Under the command of MDSU1, Navy divers recovered the missing crewmembers.

September 11, 2001—Terrorists attack the World Trade Center and Pentagon.

October, 2001—US Navy deploys to Afghanistan in support of Operation Enduring Freedom.

MK V diver in training in Tarpon Spring, Florida.

Second Class Dive School, NAB Coronado, California.

MDV Dave Gove. Old U.S. Navy Draeger recompression chamber.

Sealab II being prepared for its next day descent to the sea floor, 205' below.

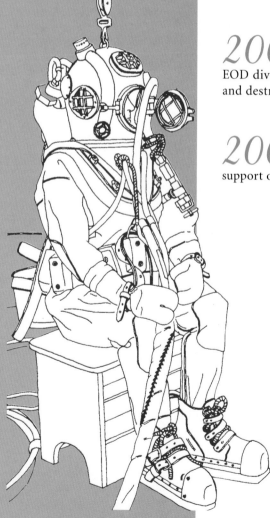

2002 MDSU2 divers recover the gun turret from the *Monitor*.

2003 US Navy SEALs deploy to Iraq in support of Operation Iraqi Freedom. Naval Special Clearance Team ONE, EOD divers, and marine mammal systems deploy to the Gulf to locate and destroy Iraqi mines.

2005 US Navy deep-sea divers, EOD divers, SEALs, and Marine RECON divers continue to deploy the world over in support of the Global War on Terrorism and a variety of other missions.

Supervisor of
Salvage & Diving

KEEPING AMERICA'S NAVY #1 IN THE WORLD

*I*f deep-sea divers represent the brawn of Navy diving, then SUPSALV can definitely be considered the brains behind the operation. The Office of the Director of Ocean Engineering, Supervisor of Salvage and Diving (SUPSALV), or 00C as it is known in the fleet, is part of Naval Sea Systems Command (NAVSEA). SUPSALV is located in the Washington Navy Yard in Washington, DC, and is responsible for all aspects of ocean engineering, including salvage, in-water ship repair, contracting, towing, diving safety, and equipment maintenance and procurement.

The staffing is generally 10 to 12 military personnel, 30 civilian personnel and one Royal Navy Exchange Officer in five support divisions:

Capt. Chris Murray 00C during the Monitor *project.*

00C1   The Management Support Division prepares and tracks contractual and financial documents and provides logistic support to the other divisions in SEA 00C.

00C2   The Salvage Operations Division handles salvage and recovery and the publication of US Navy Salvage Manuals, Salvage Engineer's Handbooks, and several other salvage-related technical manuals and instructions. 00C25 handles pollution and oil spill control operations.

00C3   The Diving Program Division is responsible for setting diving policy and approving US Navy Diving Equipment plus the publication of the US Navy Diving Manual.

00C4   The Diving Certification Division serves as the System Certification Authority for shipboard and portable hyperbaric systems.

00C5   The Underwater Ship Husbandry Division (UWSH) develops techniques, procedures, and equipment to perform in-water ship and submarine repairs and maintenance.

Obviously the Salvage division (00C2) and the Diving division (00C3) work closely together to support underwater salvage operations, so it is not unusual to have both supervisors, SUPSALV and SUPDIVE, involved in major diving operations.

*Captain James Wilkins USN
Director of Ocean Engineering
Supervisor of Salvage and Diving.*

*Captain Mark Helmkamp USN
Supervisor of Diving.*

*BMCM (MDV) Fred K. Orns,
NAVSEA Fleet Master Diver.*

*BMCM (MDV) Steve Smith,
Fleet Master Diver.*

But don't be mistaken that the Supervisors of Salvage and Diving, usually Naval Captains or Commanders, are just desk-bound administrators. Both can frequently be found on real world diving operations, taking their turn in the dive rotation alongside Second Class divers fresh out of Navy dive school.

Through 2001 and 2002, the recovery of the Civil War ironclad *Monitor* was a pet project of then SUPDIVE, Captain Chris Murray[2] who frequently made working dives to 240 feet. His predecessor, and then CO of Mobile Diving & Salvage Unit TWO (MDSU-2), Commander Barbara "Bobbie" Scholley,[3] could also be found donning a hot-water suit and MK 21 to take her turn clearing debris on the bottom.

The current Supervisor of Diving and former CO of the Navy Dive School, Captain Mark Helmkamp,[4] is another hard-core deep-sea diver and can be found diving with various commands at every opportunity. At the time of writing he was headed to Hawaii to do submarine lockouts with the SEALs.

As the Senior Chiefs and Warrant Officers have long known, Navy diving is one task where Commanders need to lead from the bottom.

ENDNOTES

1. From NAVSEA web page, www.supsalv.org
2. Captain Chris Murray was Supervisor of Diving July1999 - July 2003
3. Commander Barbara Scholley was Supervisor of Diving February 1997 - July 1999
4. Captain Mark Helmkamp took over as Supervisor of Diving July 2003

CB diver Andrew Burns hats CDR Bobbie Scholley, former Supervisor of Diving and Commanding Officer of MDSU #2 during the Monitor *Project (2001).*

Capt Bert March, SUPSALV during the Ehime Maru *Project (2001).*

U.S. Navy Diver Rates, Ratings, & Classifications

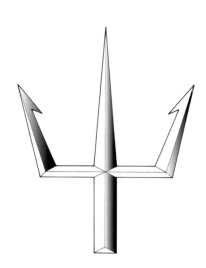

Before an aspiring Navy diver can get a foot or a fin (and do not call it a flipper!) in the door at the Navy dive school, he or she must first complete basic training for the Navy and then complete an "A" school to obtain a Navy rating. Compared to other branches of the service, the Navy has a relatively complex system of ratings, rates, ranks, and schools used in classifying enlisted personnel. These designators before their names indicate both their trade (rating) and their rank (rate) in that trade.

Although any physically fit officer or enlisted man can apply for dive school, there are specific ratings or trades that are of more value to divers than others. For the deep-sea diver, the most useful trades are those that deal with ship repair, maintenance, rigging, and engineering. These include ratings such as Boatswain's Mate (BM), Hull Technician (HT), Engineman (EN) and Machinist's Mate (MM).

For enlisted personnel hoping to go into Explosive Ordnance Disposal (EOD) — and unlike the army, all Navy EOD personnel are required to be divers — the useful ratings would be those related to ordnance: Gunner's Mate (GM), Mineman (MN), Missile Technician (MT), Sonar Technician (ST) and Electronics Technician (ET).

Sailors with training as a Hospital Corpsman (HM) would go to the diving medical technician (DMT) programs, while a Photographer's Mate (PH) may end up as a diver with a Fleet Combat Camera unit.

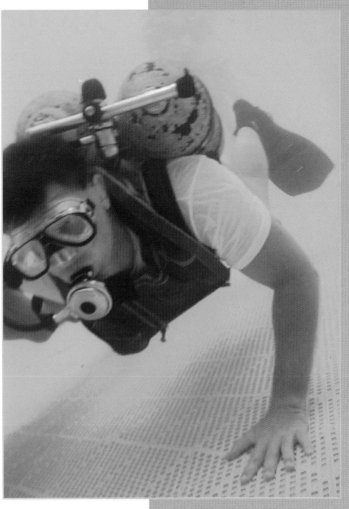

It all begins with basic scuba pool training.

Dive school applicants who have already qualified for SeaBee Construction Battalions (CB) with engineering ratings such as Builder (BU), Construction Mechanic (CM), Construction Electrician (CE), or Steelworker (SW), would be in line for construction diver training. From dive school they would graduate out to an Underwater Construction Team (UCT).

A number after that rating, for example SW2 (DV), indicates the sailor's rate of Steelworker Second Class, and the (DV) means that he is also a First Class diver. An HM1 (SEAL) would be a Hospital Corpsman First Class Petty Officer (E-6) with SEAL Teams. CPO is an E-7 Chief Petty Officer; LPO is a Lead Petty Officer; BMCS (MDV) would be a Senior Chief Boatswain's Mate, Master Diver; and watch out for the MMCM (MDV/DSWS), this would be a Master Chief Machinist Mate, Master Diver, Diving Salvage Warfare Specialist (DSWS).

Three other abbreviations often seen in the world of Navy diving are CMC — Command Master Chief, CWO — Chief Warrant Officer, and EDO — Engineering Duty Officer.

NAVY DIVER CLASSIFICATIONS

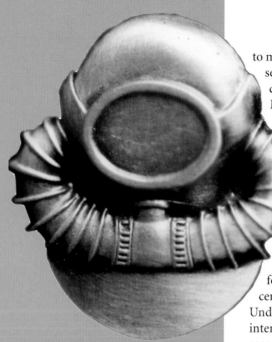

Scuba "Bubble"

There are numerous classifications of divers within the Navy designed to meet all underwater needs and mission requirements. Within the deep-sea diving community a Navy diver will begin his first tour as a second-class diver and may ultimately aspire to be a deep saturation diver or Master Diver by the end of his career, if he or she can go the distance.

In the combat diving community, divers can begin as basic scuba divers and then continue training in EOD with mixed-gas rebreathers (MK16 UBA), or in SEALs as a combatant swimmer or SEAL Delivery Vehicle (SDV) pilot. Marine Corps Reconnaissance divers and combat swimmers also fall under the supervision of US Navy diving and standards.

The following is an overview of the various classifications within the Navy and Marine Corps diving community.

SUBMARINE SCUBA DIVER. All SSNs carry a small group of SCUBA-qualified personnel for security swims prior to departing foreign ports, so the Navy maintains a number of SCUBA training centers. However, the Navy's version of a basic SCUBA (Self Contained Underwater Breathing Apparatus) certification is considerably more intense than the civilian recreational counterpart. Where a civilian recreational SCUBA program can be completed in 3 or 4 days, the Navy program is a 21-day course covering all aspects of open-circuit scuba diving, diving physics, and diving related injuries and treatment. Training evolutions include underwater work projects, search procedures, hull inspections, and qualification dives. This course can be taught at various commands and qualifies the trainee to a depth of 130 feet.

Even though sailors with just a SCUBA pin are technically divers, and often are referred to as divers, they are not considered Navy Divers until they have successfully completed Second Class (2C) dive school.

Second Class

DIVER SECOND CLASS (NEC 5343) is the entry-level classification for Navy deep-sea divers. The Second Class Diver is qualified in SCUBA, surface-supplied air diving with the MK 21 helmet and MK 20 full-face mask, and all the underwater work skills required of a fleet diver. All salvage, ship's husbandry, and construction divers begin their careers as a "Two Charlie."

SALVAGE CONSTRUCTION DEMOLITION DIVER (NEC 5375) is an advanced diver classification for salvage and construction divers. Divers are trained in military explosives and precision cutting techniques for accessing or sectioning sunken ships during wrecking-in-place operations.

DIVING MEDICAL TECHNICIAN (DMT) qualifies Hospital Corpsman (HM) — NEC 8494 — to function as a surface-supplied diving team member/diver and to handle a variety of diving related injuries such as the bends (DCS) and arterial gas embolisms (AGE). DMTs are also qualified in the use of Navy standard decompression tables and running decompression diving operations.

EOD DIVER qualifies Explosive Ordnance Disposal (EOD) team members to use SCUBA, MK-16 mixed-gas underwater breathing apparatus (UBA), or surface-supplied diving systems. Training includes underwater searches, hull inspections, small boat seamanship, introduction to underwater electronic search equipment such as the hand-held sonar, and mine counter-measures (MCM) operations.

USMC COMBATANT DIVER (MCD) qualifies Reconnaissance Marines (0321) to use USMC Open-Circuit SCUBA, and USMC Closed-

Master Diver's Conference.

Circuit (MK25) diving equipment on combat operations. Considerable training is given in underwater infiltration in accordance with current Marine Corps training and mission performance standards.

AMPHIBIOUS RECONNAISSANCE CORPSMAN qualifies SCUBA/LAR V trained Hospital Corpsman diver personnel (NEC 8403) to perform medical functions, supervise recompression chamber operations, and participate as a dive team member/diver in SCUBA and LAR V (MK25) in support of USMC Reconnaissance operations.

DIVER FIRST CLASS (NEC 5342) is the next step up the ladder and qualifies the diver to not only perform operational air diving as a dive team member, but also to plan and supervise diving operations.

HEO$_2$ MIXED-GAS DIVER qualifies First Class Divers for all aspects of surface supplied mixed-gas diving using heli-ox mixtures (HeO$_2$).

SATURATION DIVER qualifies First Class Divers for deep saturation and bell diving operations.

First Class

MASTER DIVER/MDV (NEC 5341) is the ultimate diver classification and rating for enlisted Navy personnel. A Master Diver is the living embodiment of Navy diving and is qualified to perform as a Diving Supervisor in all facets of Navy diving. Master Divers also serve as the mentors, the motivators, and the guiding force for all divers and diving support personnel under their command.

SEAL/COMBATANT SWIMMER (NEC 5326) is the Naval Special Warfare Classification for a SEAL who has graduated from the Basic Underwater Demolitions/SEAL (BUD/S) program in Coronado, California. Naval Special Warfare Command (SPECWARCOM) operates quite separately from other Naval commands but employs a significant number of Navy divers to support special operations, including Master Divers to supervise the Dive Lockers.

Master Diver

MDV Dave Gove.

BMCM (MDV) "Ragman" Radeki
(left) with author at NDSTC.

MDSU-2 Command Staff.

NAVY DIVING OFFICERS & DIVING MEDICAL OFFICERS

In many military occupations, officers command and oversee operations but are often not required to do the same physical work as the enlisted. The division of responsibility is somewhat like a civil construction project — the officers are the white-collar engineers and contractors, the Chiefs and NCOs are the work foremen, and the enlisted troops are the labor force. In the world of Navy diving it is quite different.

Officers are not only required to go through training that is every bit as grueling as their enlisted counterparts, they are motivated to participate in all aspects of real-world diving operations. In fact, many officers will welcome the opportunity to get wet and put their hard earned skills to the test.

SEAL

However, the primary responsibility of a Diving Officer is to help plan and supervise diving operations. The officer can only dive if there is another Diving Officer to take his or her place on the deck.

BASIC DIVING OFFICER (BDO) is the initial classification for US Naval officers qualifying them to serve as a working diver as well as the operational Diving Officer. BDOs wear the gold hard-hat pin and have the 1160 designator until they qualify as a Surface Warfare Officer (SWO), at which time they pick up the 1140 Naval Special Operations designator (not the same as SPECWAR).

SALVAGE DIVING OFFICER qualifies the Naval Officer in all phases of salvage operations. This month-long advanced course provides BDOs follow-on training in salvage seamanship, salvage machinery, salvage computation, and practical experience in conducting and supervising salvage operations.

HYPERBARIC MEDICAL OFFICER (HMO) is designed to provide Medical Officers with the basic training to perform as a medical advisor for hyperbaric treatments and to evaluate divers and diver candidates prior to diving.

MEDICAL DEPARTMENT DIVING OFFICER is designed to provide qualified Medical Officers with the training necessary to operate with the dive team as a consultant, team member, or diver during surface-supplied diving operations.

DIVING MEDICAL OFFICER (DMO) On completion of this course graduates are certified US Navy Divers and certified or familiarized on every diving system in use in the military. While intended for Undersea Medical Officer Candidates and Army Special Forces Physicians, the course is open to physicians from all branches of service.

NAVAL SPECIAL WARFARE OFFICER. To become a SEAL, Naval officers are required to complete BUD/S training alongside their enlisted counterparts. Upon graduation they reserve the 1180 NEC designator as a probationary special warfare officer. When they become fully qualified SEAL officers they receive the 1130 career designator and the coveted gold Trident.

DMO LT Julianna Lippert
working surface coms on the
Monitor *project.*

Surface-supplied diver training.

*Guidon for Basic
Diving Officers course.*

U.S. Navy Diving Equipment

DEEP SEA DIVING EQUIPMENT

Though now retired by the Navy, any discussion of diving equipment would be incomplete without tracing the origins of Navy deep-sea diving back to the MK V heavy gear. To this day, the polished copper and brass MK V helmets found in the reception areas of every diving command continue to conjure up images of high adventure from a bygone era. Today, the danger and adventure are still out there, but the copper and brass have been replaced by fiberglass and stainless steel.

Based first on the British Navy's Davis Six-Bolt Admiralty Pattern helmet manufactured by Siebe-Gorman and influenced by early Schrader and Morse helmets, the classic MK V Deep Sea Diving Dress was introduced by the Navy's Bureau of Construction & Repair in 1917 and soon after was adopted by the Navy for all salvage and diving operations.

Beginning in1913 there were several refinements made to existing commercial hats made by Morse and Schrader, not surprisingly influenced by Schrader designs, since Navy diving development was working out of the Schrader facilities. The Navy also specified the addition of a battery operated electric telephone, greatly improving communications. However, it was the salvage of the submarine USS *F-4* in 1915 from 304 feet of water off Hawaii that established the practical limits for air diving.

In 1927 the weight of the MK V was reduced to 56 pounds (30 for the helmet and 26 for the breastplate assembly) to improve diver comfort and mobility with little change in the design after that date. However, the diver had more than just the weight of the helmet assembly to contend with. The basic diving dress was constructed from vulcanized rubber, friction calendar-coated between an outer cotton twill layer and an inner layer of a similar material. Heavy chafing patches were cemented to the areas of the highest wear, bringing the complete weight of the suit in at about 20 pounds.

The weightbelt and cross-strapped harness were constructed of double-backed waterproof leather and weighed approximately 84 pounds, made up of individual seven and a half pound lead blocks. The shoes, weighing approximately seventeen and a half pounds each, were constructed of leather or canvas uppers with a hardwood sole, a lead lower sole and a cast bronze toe-guard. With between 200 and 250 pounds of equipment, the diver was definitely dependent on his tenders to not only dress him in and out but also for assistance to and from the water.

At the start of WW II two companies were manufacturing the MK V—Morse and Schrader, but after the attack on Pearl Harbor in December 1941, DESCO and Miller-Dunn also began manufacturing the MK V. DESCO began producing the MK V sometime in 1942 and was manufacturing 8 helmets a day by 1945. Between 1942 and 1945, DESCO produced some 3,000 helmets, and in the post war years there was such a glut of helmets that one could reportedly purchase a new helmet for a little over one hundred dollars. Today that same helmet retails for four to five thousand dollars.

The MK V, however heavy and cumbersome at the time, provided the diver with a safe working environment,

MK V diver.

Mark V - Desco 1944.

MK12 SSDS.

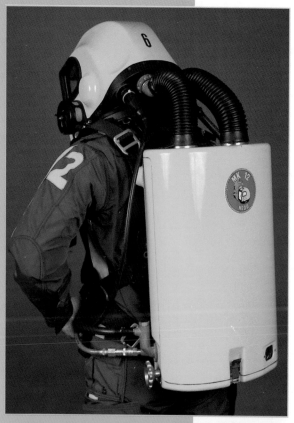

MK12 semi-closed circuit recirculator pack made by General Electric.

not only protecting him from the cold but also from pollutants and infections. The helmet had adequate communications and a built-in air reserve, so it is no surprise that the MK V heavy gear served with distinction and survived in the Navy dive lockers until the mid-eighties, to be replaced by the more advanced MK 12.

In 1939, Lt. "Swede" Momsen's EDU and salvage divers proved the value of mixed-gas diving techniques in the recovery of the USS *Squalus* from 243 fsw. Based on this success, the Navy developed a re-circulating MK V Mod 1 for mixed-gas diving. However, as seen in the movie "Men of Honor," the helmet and breastplate were extremely heavy, weighing in at over 100 pounds, nearly twice the weight of the MK V air hat. (Current production Desco Navy Helium MK V Mod 1 with the canister is 93 pounds.)

In the forties, for surface-supplied diving and as a lightweight alternative to the MK V, the Navy went to a triangular-shaped mask named after its inventor, "Jack Browne," which had a standard depth limit of 60 feet and a maximum of 90 feet. This simple mask was in service until the late 70s and early 80s, however the Jack Browne was a free-flow mask and did not support a voice communications system. Communications from the diver were effected by a series of line-pull signals on the umbilical to the topside tender.

The current lightweight diving mask used by Navy divers is the MK 20 Aga mask made by Interspiro, with OTS two-way communications and a standard working depth limit of 60 feet. These lightweight masks have a low profile so are well suited to work in tight spaces such as submarine ballast compartments.

In the late 60s and early 70s, several Navy commands began using the Kirby-Morgan Bandmask (KMB-8) long before these new and sturdier masks had been formally approved for Navy use. In 1976 the Navy approved the Kirby-Morgan Bandmask, designated the US Navy Mask MK-1 Mod 0, for use as a lightweight diving mask. This was the Navy's version of the then-popular civilian model KMB-10, in use with many commercial divers.

Based on Navy diving regulations, the MK-1 could be used to 60 feet without a come-home bottle, 130 feet with a come-home emergency bailout bottle, and 190 feet with an open bell. The MK-1 Mod 0 Lightweight, Mixed-Gas Diving Outfit was also approved and used for dives to 300 fsw on helium-oxygen.

As all these developments in surface-supplied diving progressed, there was also a greater interest in deep mixed-gas bell diving. By the late seventies, the MK V was still in use by Navy divers, giving them a normal working limit on air to 190 feet, or down to 250 feet for 90 minutes on Exceptional Exposure diving operations. However, in 1978 and 1979, NEDU was developing four new systems: the Mark 11 semi-closed circuit system, the Mark 14 "push/pull" to conserve helium and extend dive times on saturation dives, the MK 15 UBA mixed gas rebreather, and the MK 12 SSDS.

MK12 divers being brought aboard.

The MK 12 Surface-Supported Diving System (SSDS) came onto the scene in the late seventies and by 1980 had replaced the heavy MK V Mod 1 gas hat for deep mixed-gas diving. Then in 1985 the MK 12 was officially approved for all Fleet diving to replace the standard MK V heavy gear, marking the death of an era in Navy diving. The MK V dress would be relegated to display-only at the various diving commands and museums.

The MK 12 SSDS was very much a "system" approach to diving, with several integrated components. In addition to the helmet assembly, consisting of a shell and base, the dress assembly is comprised of a dry suit, coverall out garment, jocking harness, pocket weights, lightweight boots, and gloves. Support equipment included the umbilical, welding shields, flow meter, test set and tools, spare parts, a repair kit, and a re-circulator assembly for mixed-gas diving. A basic MK 12 diving package contained three helmets, three 200-foot umbilicals, and three 600-foot umbilicals.

However, even with all the research and development that went into the MK 12, it was not a very successful design, making the MK-1 bandmask more efficient for both gas and bell diving. Then in 1990 the MK-1 Mod 0 bandmask was replaced by the MK 21, a helmet based on Kirby-Morgan's DSI Superlite 17B.

Three years later, in 1993, the MK 12 was replaced by the MK 21 for all air and mixed-gas diving applications. The only item of the MK 12 system that survives to this day in Navy dive lockers is the blue outer garment with its distinctive gold strip. This suit makes excellent chafing gear and is valued by Navy divers for its numerous pockets that will hold tools, nuts, bolts, shackles, and extra weights.

Tender and MK12 diver showing jocking harness.

MK12 divers exiting the diving stage.

Even though the MK 21 had replaced the MK 12 and the MK 1 bandmask, the Navy was still in need of a lightweight diving mask. Put into service around 1988 and then adopted by the Navy in the early nineties, the MK 22 Mod 0 Bandmask was the Navy's version of the successful DSI-18B bandmask, with a few modifications to the dump valve. The MK 22 bandmask was introduced as a lightweight alternative to the MK 21 and for use by the stand-by diver in a diving bell. Being a bandmask with a neoprene hood and spider straps, it is easier for one diver to don and doff without assistance from a tender.

The MK 21, known in the commercial diving field as a Kirby-Morgan SuperLite 17B, is constructed with a fiberglass shell that is weighted for neutral buoyancy, so it does not require an uncomfortable crotch-grabbing jocking system to stop the helmet floating up on the diver. It also has a demand regulator, greatly improving gas efficiency and eliminating much of the noise and communication interference associated with free-flow helmets.

For working at night, the MK 21 can be fitted with the Divers Helmet Mounted Lighting System (DHMLS), and a Divers Underwater Camera Television System (DUCTS) can be added so that the diving supervisor and attending engineers can see on topside video exactly what the diver is working on.

As with all surface-supplied diving rigs, the MK 21 diver is connected to the surface by an umbilical that serves several functions. First and foremost, the umbilical carries air or mixed-gas to the diver, which is fed through a topside control panel from either a low-pressure (LP) compressor or gas storage bottles (CHAOS air racks). The second component of the umbilical is a "commo or coms" line that gives the diver clear, two-way communications with the surface. Also included in the bundle is a pneumo-fathometer, or pneumo hose, that allows the diving control system (DCS) operator to monitor the diver's depth. In addition to all these, the umbilical can have a hose to feed hot water for the diver's hot water suit, plus a video cable and a power cable for the helmet-mounted light.

For added safety and security, the umbilical is attached to a diving harness that may also carry the diver's emergency gas supply (EGS), commonly called a bailout or come-home bottle. The Navy harnesses are constructed from exceptionally strong webbing, riveted together with stainless steel D-rings to serve as umbilical attachment points. The two types of harness mostly commonly seen on diving jobs today are the black Atlantic Diving Equipment versions and blue Miller harnesses.

As can be seen thoughout this book, the yellow MK 21 diving helmet with its kidney-shaped face-plate is the signature piece of equipment for all Navy deep-sea divers today, just as the MK V was for their predecessors. The MK 20 mask is the lightweight alternative for surface-supplied diving, and the MK 22 bandmask is still used by the stand-by diver for bell diving operations.

Not to be too easily relegated to history or forgotten, it is still a source of considerable pride for a Navy diver to be able to claim that he had been trained on the venerable MK V heavy gear.

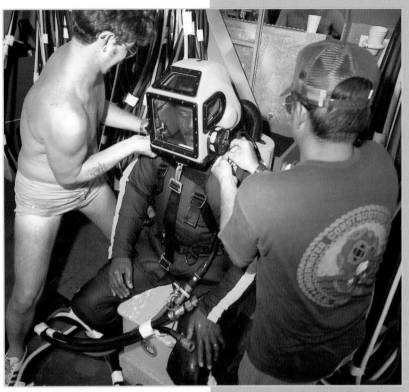

"Hatting" the diver.

MK21 with mounted video and lights.

MK 21, the Navy version of the KM Superlite 17.

Unfortunately, the Navy no longer dives the MK V, so the polished helmets and dusty suits now adorn the offices and hallways of virtually every diving command in the Navy. They stand as silent testament to a long history of courage and hard work, and a reminder to new divers of the proud traditions they must strive to maintain.

FLY-AWAY DIVING SYSTEMS

US Navy divers can be called to any part of the globe on a moment's notice to support combat operations or recover a downed aircraft. However, going by ship is often too slow, so Navy dive teams must have diving systems designed for rapid deployment by air.

The modern deep-sea dive teams, such as Mobile Diving & Salvage Units (MDSU) and Underwater Construction Teams (UCT), are very much air-mobile, even referring to their teams as Air Dets or Detachments. To facilitate rapid deployment and ease of use, pre-packaged

NDSTC hat shop where current MK21 helmets are maintained and repaired.

Former Navy saturation and EDU diver Mike Ward, currently President of Dive Lab in Panama City, supporting commercial and military diving research and development.

MKIII diving console.

Checking the inline filters and reducer on ASRA.

Air supply rack assembly (ASRA) and chamber at MDSU-ONE in Hawaii.

surface-support diving systems have been developed and containerized. These modular systems are referred to as "Fly-Aways," consisting of a number of components such as the Fly-Away Dive Locker (FADL) and the Fly-Away Diving System (FADS).

The FADS MK III can be either an Air System or a Mixed-Gas System, and consists of a MK 3 Lightweight Diving System console and volume tank assembly (CHAOS air racks), with interface umbilicals to connect the systems, a low-pressure (LP) diving compressor, three diving umbilicals, and three MK 21 helmets (commonly referred to as "hats").

There is considerable flexibility built into the fly-away diving systems based on the mission configuration matrix. A package may also include Fly-Away Recompression Chambers (FARCC) for prolonged or deep diving operations.

The US Navy Fly-Away Recompression Chamber (FARCC) is a 200 cubic foot, double-lock steel chamber that is depth rated to 225 fsw and US Navy certified. Mounted on a life support skid (LSS) and weighing in at 13,400 pounds fully outfitted, it comes with its own diesel generator, high-pressure air compressor, and external environmental conditioning system.

Another option for recompression chambers are the more mobile Transportable Recompression Chamber Systems (TRCS). These are smaller, trailer mounted, two-piece recompression chambers that can be assembled on site.

For deep diving operations, deeper than the 190-foot limit for air diving, the dive team will deploy the Fly-Away Mixed-Gas System (FMGS).

Explosive Ordnance Disposal teams also have their own dive lockers and diving systems, such as the EOD MK 1 Mod 0 Mobile Support Facility consisting of a FARCC/LSS and an EOD FADL fly-away dive locker.

SCUBA & REBREATHER EQUIPMENT DEVELOPMENT

Compared to surface-supplied deep-sea diving equipment, which can be traced back to the 1800s, the self-contained underwater breathing apparatus (SCUBA), as we know it today, is a relatively new invention. The first demand-type regulator that could supply the diver with compressed air as he breathed, as opposed to earlier free-flow systems, was developed by French Naval Lieutenant Cousteau and engineer Emile Gagnan in 1943.

Using Cousteau's Aqua Lung after several hundred work-up dives, Frederic Dumas made a record dive to 307 feet in 1947 — the same year that the US Navy became interested in the Aqua-Lung equipment for evaluation and to expand the diving capabilities of the Underwater Demolition Teams. Although open-circuit SCUBA was useful for working divers, it was immediately evident that the telltale bubbles emitted by the SCUBA equipment were a dead give-away for combat divers.

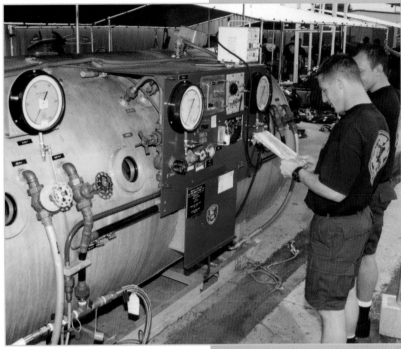

MDSU divers operating an older double-lock aluminum recompression chamber.

The earliest American closed-circuit unit, adopted by Office of Strategic Services (OSS) in the early forties, was the Lambertsen MK III LARU. In 1940, Dr. Lambertsen, now considered "The Father of US Combat Swimming," had developed the Lambertson Lung (LARU), along with the concept of forming teams of underwater assault swimmers. In 1942 the OSS established a maritime unit and recruited Dr Lambertsen, a reserve Captain in the US Army Medical Corps, to create an underwater operations program and develop the supporting training methods and hardware.

While the OSS was developing combat swimmer capabilities, Lieutenant Commander Draper Kauffman, "The Father of Demolitions," was tasked with organizing and training the early Naval Combat Demolitions Units. This also opened the door to the concept of pre-assault reconnaissance and beach marking teams. But at that time the teams were still primarily surface swimmers.

By the time OSS swimmer groups were being absorbed into UDT teams in 1944, the Lambertsen rebreather had evolved into the LARU MK 10.

It wasn't until after the war that Lieutenant Commander Doug Fane, CO of UDT 2, was tasked with developing a sub-surface capability and to apply SCUBA to UDT operations. At that time, the only two units available were the early "Jack Browne" used in UDT basic training at Ft. Pierce and the Lambertsen Amphibious Respiratory Unit used by the OSS.

Closed-circuit oxygen rebreather.

Air supply rack assembly (ASRA).

MKIII lightweight air system.

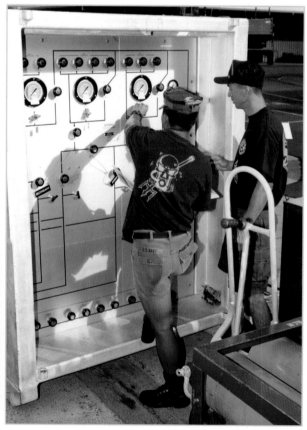

Central panel for ASRA.

OTS diver recall system.

By the 50s, the UDTs had three units to chose from — the Aqualung, the Italian Pirelli and the early German Drager. It wasn't until 1962 that the first US closed-circuit unit, the Emerson, became operational. Concurrently, a semi-closed-circuit mixed-gas scuba unit was developed and designated the MK 5, but it was not a successful unit.

In 1964 the Navy adopted the MK 6 UBA semi-closed circuit rebreather for combat swimmers and EOD. This unit had a maximum depth limit of 200 fsw and served the Navy well until 1979, when the MK 6 was replaced by the MK 15 — a mixed-gas closed-circuit rebreather.

In search of a fully closed-circuit shallow water rebreather for bubble-free special operations, the Navy officially adopted the Draeger LAR V in 1982, designating it the MK 25 Closed-Circuit Underwater Breathing Apparatus. This replaced the Emerson-Lambertson rebreather.

In a push to improve the MK 15 mixed-gas rebreather, in 1985 a low-magnetic sensor-controlled MK 16 mixed-gas, closed-circuit UBA was approved for EOD and SEAL applications.

Navy diver works to restore an old MKV for a command display.

The most recent up-grade in rebreather development is the addition of M 48 full-face mask designed and manufactured by Kirby-Morgan. This rugged mask has a detachable oral-nasal mouthpiece that can accommodate both open-circuit regulators and rebreather hoses.

Another recent addition to the Navy's dive locker is a decompression computer called the NDC (Navy Dive Computer). Running tables for basic square profile dives still works fine, but for a SEAL SDV operator, who may begin his DDS spin-ups and approach on air, then change to MK16 mixed-gas or even 100% O_2 during the operation, a computer capable of computing multiple levels and gases was essential.

In October 2000, NEDU recommended approval of the Cochran NAVY for SEAL use; then in January 2001, the Supervisor of Diving & Salvage authorized the use of this dive computer (DC) by selected SEAL units. The Navy's first decompression computer dive was conducted by Bravo Platoon of SDV Team One on 13 January 2001 in the waters off Barber's Point in Hawaii.[1]

Conventional open-circuit SCUBA equipment is still widely used in Navy diving today, especially for administrative activities and where the divers need untethered mobility and freedom of movement. Equipment from several manufacturers has been tested and approved for Navy use, giving the individual commands and Navy divers considerable flexibility in the equipment they dive.

ENDNOTES

1. Article by CAPT Frank K. Butler, M.D., Director of Biomedical Research, Naval Special Warfare.

U.S. Navy
Experimental
Diving Unit

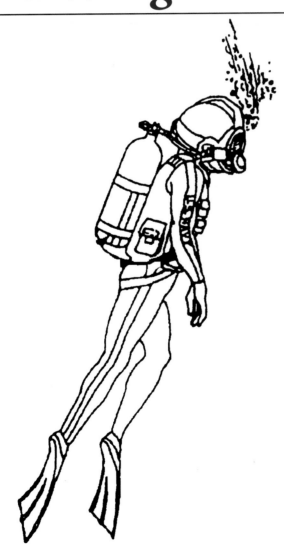

Capt. George F. Bond,
"Papa Topside."

NEDU VISION

To be the most credible and respected research, development, test, and evaluation center for diving and the focal point of leadership for bio-medical/bio-engineering solutions for undersea military operations.

True to this vision, the US Navy Experimental Diving Unit is one of, if not the, world's premier diving research facility. Located in Panama City, Florida, NEDU serves as the hub of all military diving research and equipment test & evaluation.

BRIEF HISTORY OF NEDU

NEDU was first established in 1927 at the Washington Navy Yard where all aspects of Navy diving research were undertaken. From 1930 through 1940, NEDU scientists, engineers, and divers pioneered mixed-gas heliox diving procedures along with submarine escape and rescue systems.

NEDU was instrumental in developing the USN Diving Manual with continuous revisions and the publishing of the USN Standard Decompression Tables (first published in 1956).

The divers, technicians, and scientists of EDU were also heavily involved in the validation of saturation diving techniques with the Genesis Program (1957–1963), followed by the Man-in-the-Sea Program and Sealab projects (1964–1969). (See Chapter 19.)

In 1975 NEDU was moved to Panama City to co-locate with the Ocean Simulation Facility (OSF) that had been built in 1972. From 1975 NEDU focused their resources on saturation diving procedures and supported Naval Special Warfare (SPECWAR) and EOD with development of low signature diving systems, closed-circuit rebreathers, fleet diving equipment, and procedures for both salvage and underwater ship's husbandry.

In 1985 NEDU became the In-Service Engineering Agent for Diving Systems supplying Joint Service Support for the US Marine Corps, Army, and Air Force.

NEDU in Panama City, Florida.

U.S. Navy personnel transfer capsule (PTC) from a deep saturation diving system.

NEDU TODAY

The Navy Experimental Diving Unit is a field activity of NAVSEA, which reports directly to the Director of Ocean Engineering, Salvage & Diving (SEA 00C). NEDU is a tenant command of the Coastal Systems Station (CSS) (Now Naval Surface Warfare Center Panama City [NSWC-PC]), located in Panama City and a convenient neighbor of the Naval Diving & Salvage Training Center, making the facility the Navy's center of excellence for diving research, development, testing, evaluation, and training. CSS is a comprehensive Navy research and development laboratory focused on amphibious warfare, coastal operations, diving, life support, and mine warfare.[1]

The NEDU team is composed of approximately 160 highly qualified and experienced diving officers, scientists, medical professionals, military divers, and support personnel. Divers are drawn from all diving communities: Sea-Air-Land team (SEALs), Explosive Ordnance Disposal (EOD), Salvage, Saturation, Seabees, Engineering Duty Officers, Undersea Medical Officers (UMO). The team includes a professional staff of eight Diving Medical Officers (DMO), eleven Ph.D. scientists, eight engineers, and a number of other science-degreed professionals. EDU also provides on-call service 24/7 for technical consultation for the Navy's UMOs.

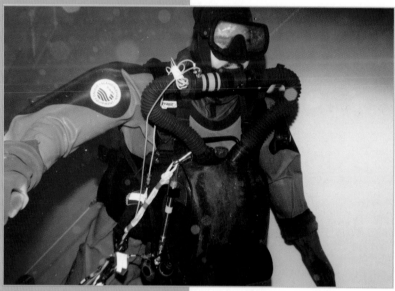

NEDU diver in a cold water rebreather study.

NEDU diver in an endurance rebreather study.

NEDU DIVERS

The Navy divers assigned to NEDU participate in all facets of Unit operations, from running the hyperbaric facilities to serving as test subjects for both medical and biomechanical research. Use of mechanical breathing machines and drawing scientific extrapolations from data derived by artificial means have limits and only take diving research so far. From there, the equipment and procedures must be evaluated under real-world conditions on human guinea pigs, but in a relatively safe, controlled scientific environment.

The type of experiments that require the participation of divers include the development of decompression procedures, evaluation of ergonomics of underwater equipment, study of breathing characteristics of closed-circuit diving rigs, and finding the limits of human endurance under a variety of carefully monitored conditions.

For example, divers may be required to perform in very warm waters (>90°F) as found in the Arabian Gulf regions, or very cold waters (<40°F) as found on a North Korean approach profile. The NEDU researchers study the divers and their equipment to see how performance is adversely affected at these temperatures, how the diving equipment functions, the duration of the carbon-dioxide absorbent in closed-circuit rigs, and the forms of thermal protection that can be developed for the divers and their diving equipment.

These types of conditions can be simulated in the test tanks and chambers at NEDU, allowing the command to collect data and validate diving procedures in a controlled environment. The results and recommendations can then be disseminated to frontline units tasked with operating under extreme conditions for special operations, EOD, or salvage.

The divers assigned to NEDU, drawn from all classifications of Navy diving, are some of the best and brightest in the fleet. But there is a downside to being on staff at NEDU as an experimental diver. Apart from being taken to the very limits of physical endurance during testing, the divers must submit to several rather invasive procedures as the medical staff inserts a variety of data-collection probes into the divers' bodies.

Exertion study.

Researchers need these probes and sensors to monitor the divers' vital signs and physiological reactions to the experiments. In addition, divers may be required to give blood and urine samples before, after, and sometimes during experiments to better monitor the divers' condition. This vital data not only enhances fleet diver and combat swimmer safety, it allows NEDU to make recommendations and improvements to the full range of Navy diving equipment and the manner in which it is employed.

Unmanned test chamber.

NEDU & NAVAL SPECIAL WARFARE

NEDU has had a long and rewarding relationship with the Naval Special Warfare (NSW) community that has benefited both groups. The SEALs at NSW are always looking to push their operational capabilities to the limits, and NEDU is more than happy to help these motivated young men find those limits. Over the past two decades, NEDU research has significantly extended the diving capabilities of the SEALs and given them direction on how to better execute their missions with a greater degree of safety.

The research that NEDU undertook to establish the depth and time limits of 100% oxygen rebreather diving was probably the most comprehensive and exhaustive study ever undertaken. Over a four-year period and several hundred experimental dives, many taking the divers to the point of convulsion

Ocean simulator facility "wet tank."

EX-14 Helmet.

and even CNS oxygen toxicity, NEDU was able to make recommendations that would allow the SEALs to greatly extend their mission-driven depth and time capabilities.

Two of the lead researchers in this and many other NSW projects were Captain Frank Butler, MC[2], a Diving Medical Officer and former UDT & SEAL platoon commander, and Captain Ed Thalman, MC. Both also worked on the development of diving procedures for the MK 15 and MK 16 mixed-gas UBAs.

Another significant contribution to the SPECWAR community was multi-level dive procedures for combat swimmers. Combined with the research on diving multiple gas mixtures on a single operation, or repetitive operational dives, NEDU came up with the current issue NAVY dive computer (NDC) being used by SEALs and SDV teams. The computer's algorithm (VVAL 18) is also based on earlier decompression research done at NEDU by Captain Thalman.

Along with decompression issues, the effect of extreme temperature has long been a concern for the SEALs, particularly when it has a negative impact on human performance and mission capability. NEDU has done numerous studies on ways to assist the diver under extreme conditions ranging from evaluating dry suits and thermal protection, to hydration and nutrition, to better protecting the diving equipment from the environment. Many of these tests necessitate SEALS and NEDU divers to be subjected to frigid 35-degree waters for three to six hours at a stint.

Every time a new piece of equipment has come into the NSW inventory, whether it was LAR Vs, MK 16s, SDVs, DDS, and now ASDS, NEDU has been there to do the research, answer the questions, and write the protocols. None of this ground breaking research would have been possible without the courage of the NEDU divers and the dedication of a select group of researchers.

NEDU FACILITIES

OCEAN SIMULATION FACILITY (OSF)

The OSF chamber simulates ocean conditions to a maximum pressure equivalent of 2,250 feet seawater (fsw) and any salinity level found in the oceans. The chamber complex consists of a 55,000 gallon wet chamber positioned under five interconnected dry living/working chambers totaling 3,300 cubic feet. Wet and dry chamber temperature can be set from 28°F to 104°F.

The OSF is equipped with state-of-the-art data acquisition capability and can accommodate a wide range of experiments, including diver biomedical studies, complex man-machine testing, and small submersible vehicles in the wet chamber.

The dry chambers function much like a conventional saturation diving system, allowing for saturations dives in the OSF for over 30 days of continuous exposure. Instead of being transported to depth by a diving bell, the divers in the dry chambers are able to drop down through a

Diver with EX-14 and hot water suit.

OSF and saturation control room.

transfer trunk and into the massive wet chamber of the OSF. These diver excursions from the dry chambers allow for man and equipment testing underwater and at depth over extended periods.

As with any saturation diving system, the dry chambers provide a comfortable environment where diver-subjects live when not performing diving excursions in the wet chamber. The dry chamber is also capable of altitude simulation studies to 150,000 feet.

UNMANNED TEST FACILITY

The unmanned test facility is equipped with state-of-the-art data acquisition instruments, 3 breathing machines (which simulate diver's breathing pattern), and mannequins. This facility's hyperbaric chamber complex is available for unmanned testing to 1,640 fsw over a temperature range of 28°F to 110°F. Testing performed includes freeze studies, work on breathing tests, carbon dioxide absorbent duration, and oxygen consumption tests for closed circuit Underwater Breathing Apparatus (UBA). After tests are conducted, ANU (authorized for Navy use) approval recommendations for equipment may be issued.

Hatch to "wet pot."

TEST POOL

The test pool is a 15-foot deep pool capable of a temperature range of 34°F to 105°F. Equipped with state-of-the-art data acquisition instruments, the test pool is used for conducting a wide range of studies including diver physiological testing, manned diving equipment, and small submersible vehicle evaluations.

ENVIRONMENTAL CHAMBER

The environmental chamber is capable of simulating a broad range of temperatures (0°F to 130°F), humidity (5% to 95%), and wind conditions (0 to 20 mph). The chamber is instrumented to conduct physiology studies and testing of diving equipment and small submersible vehicles.

TECHNICAL LIBRARY

NEDU houses one of the world's largest diving technical libraries, with over 120,000 documents on the history, engineering, and medical aspects of diving. Much of the information pertains to the original development of various diving tables, etc. Researchers from around the world, both inside and outside the diving community, use the information resources of the library.

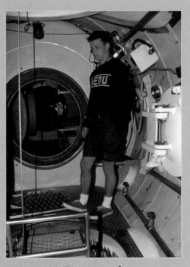

Entry trunk to wet pot.

Rebreather studies.

ENDNOTES

1.   NEDU command webpage.
2.   At time of writing, Captain Butler, MC, is the Director of Biomedical Research for the Naval Special Warfare Command.

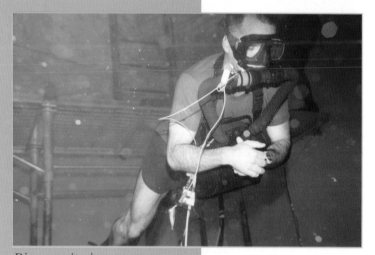

Diver monitoring.

Test pool.

MDV Ramos' NEDU certificate. Ramos made a 945' satruation dive off of San Clemente Island in 1972/1973.

Naval Diving & Salvage Training Center

PERFORMANCE UNDER PRESSURE

HISTORY OF NAVY DIVE SCHOOL

After every large war, the stay-at-home politicians sharpen their pencils and begin to whittle away at the military budget. All branches of the armed services invariable suffer severe cutbacks in both men and material, so it comes as no surprise that after WW I (1914–1918) Navy diving programs had diminished to the point that by 1925 the Navy had only 20 divers qualified to go deeper than 90 feet.

In 1927, to remedy this operational deficiency, the Naval School of Diving & Salvage (NSDS), more commonly referred to as the Navy Deep Sea Diving School, was re-established at the Washington Navy Yard. Then to consolidate Navy diving assets, the Experimental Diving Unit (EDU) was also moved to the Navy Yard from Pittsburgh the same year.

When the passenger liner *Normandie* caught fire alongside New York City's Pier 88, the huge amounts of water pumped during fire-fighting efforts caused the ship to capsize. To take advantage of the training value in salvaging this ship, and in addition to NSDS at the Washington Navy Yard, the Naval Training School (Salvage) was established in New York in September, 1942. Then in 1946, Naval Training School (Salvage) was moved from New York to Bayonne, New Jersey, as portrayed in the Hollywood feature "Men of Honor," where Carl Brashear attended Second Class dive school in 1954.

From the 50s to the 80s there were numerous diving programs run at various Naval commands, including Scuba and Second Class diver schools in Little Creek, Virginia; New London, Connecticut; 32nd Street, San Diego; and Pearl Harbor, Hawaii.

In 1980, under the cognizance of the Chief of Naval Education and Training (CNET), the current Navy dive school was established as the Naval Diving & Salvage Training Center (NDSTC) in Panama City, Florida. However, a few Second Class dive schools continued to operate at outside commands into the late eighties, and Submarine Scuba schools are still run at commands such as Pearl Harbor, Hawaii.

In 2000, under the supervision of the school's commanding officer, CDR Mark Helmkamp, the Navy commemorated the contribution that Admiral Momsen had made to Navy diving by dedicating the main building as "VADM Charles 'Swede' Momsen Hall."

Former COs of NDSTC: CDR Jon D. Kurtz (2002–2004) and CDR Helmkamp (2000–2002).

Momsen memorial.

NDSTC TRAINING FACILITIES

NDSTC offers a variety of diver training environments, including an Olympic-sized pool, welding and burning tanks, an ascent tower, pressure chambers, dockside training areas, and underwater work projects. The school's two recently delivered $7 million, 131-foot aluminum dive boats, Yard Diving Tenders YTD-17 *Neptune* and YTD-18 *Poseidon*, also give direct access to open water diving in St. Andrews Bay and the Gulf of Mexico. With diesel-driven water-jet drives and through-hull thrusters, these vessels are capable of 18 knots, can support both air and mixed-gas diving, and are the Navy's newest class of diving support vessel.

NDSTC's 155,000-square-foot facility includes an administrative block, modern classrooms for academic programs, lab areas for "hands-on" equipment training, a large pool for physical training and basic scuba skills, three indoor training tanks, and three Pressure Vessel Assemblies (PVAs).

The PVAs are very sophisticated multi-lock chambers and vertical wet-pots that allow year-round training, deep qualification diving to 190 feet on air or 300 feet on HeO_2, emergency recompression treatments, and diving candidate pressure evaluations. The facility also has a 347,000-cubic-foot gas farm to support hyperbaric diving operations and a medical facility with limited laboratory and emergency capabilities.[1]

Aerial view of NDSTC.

NAVY DIVER TRAINING

Since completion in 1980, thousands of pre-selected US and international students from all branches of the armed forces have been trained in diving and ship salvage at NDSTC. All students, if they expect to graduate, are required to demonstrate a level of comfort while performing a variety of tasks underwater. These training tasks, called projects, are designed to test the students' ability to function efficiently in an alien environment while wearing cumbersome diving equipment.

One of the most difficult facets of training for the young trainees is the academics, contributing to a high

NDSTC command headquarters.

percentage of the washouts. Academically, students will be trained in the basic gas laws as they relate to diving, human physiology and diving medicine, recompression chamber operations, dive planning, salvage mathematics, and salvage operations. The classroom routine is very demanding and requires the total commitment of every student.

To eliminate potentially weak individuals before they are committed to more dangerous deepwater operations, diver training at NDSTC is arduous and stressful by design. It demands considerable effort, both physical and mental. The gold-shirted instructors set a high standard, but as the school literature states, "with a positive attitude and the basic required physical ability, the student will be able to meet the challenge with confidence."

As of this writing, NDSTC had a staff of 160 males and 10 females processing about 1,400 students per year in twenty-two different programs running 5–26 weeks in length. At any given time there are 150–200 students on board, classed-up in their various diving specialties, which include:

- Second Class Diver (2C), covering Scuba, MK 20, and MK 21
- Basic Underwater Construction, which includes 2nd Class Diver Training
- Basic Diving Officer (BDO)
- EOD Diver, working with the MK 16 rebreather
- Marine Combat Diver (MCD) working with SCUBA and MK25
- Amphibious Reconnaissance Corpsman
- Diving Medical Technician (DMT)
- Diving Medical Officer (DMO)

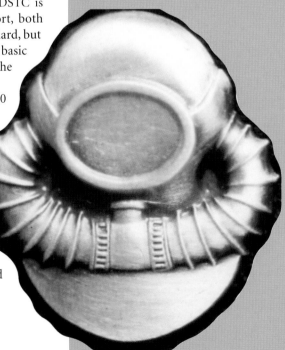

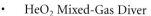

- HeO$_2$ Mixed-Gas Diver
- First Class Diver (1C)
- Master Diver Evaluations
- Saturation Diver

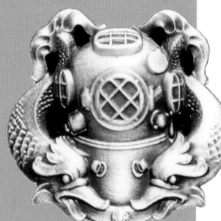

First Class

SUBMARINE SCUBA DIVER is the Navy's version of a basic SCUBA certification but considerably more intense than its civilian recreational counterpart. Where a civilian SCUBA program can be completed in 3 or 4 days, the Navy program is a 21-day course covering all aspects of open-circuit SCUBA diving, diving physics, diving related injuries, and treatment. Training evolutions include underwater work projects, search procedures, hull inspections, and qualification dives. This course can be taught at various commands and qualifies the trainee to a depth of 60 feet.

DIVER SECOND CLASS (2C) is the entry-level program for most Navy deep-sea diver applicants. Second Class Diver is a 100-day course providing instruction and training in surface-supplied air diving and SCUBA diving techniques, along with underwater repair, salvage, and search procedures. Instruction includes diving physics and medicine, scuba and surface supported diving systems, underwater tools and work techniques, and underwater cutting and welding procedures. This course qualifies trainees to a maximum depth of 190 feet.

BASIC UNDERWATER CONSTRUCTION (2C) is a 115-day course that includes everything in the 2C program but focuses more on construction skills and related tools than on ship husbandry and salvage. Students learn the skills required to operate underwater hydraulic tools, surveying equipment and small boats, how to place underwater concrete, inspect waterfront facilities and perform underwater excavation, and master the principles and techniques for precision underwater demolition.

Second Class

ADVANCED UNDERWATER CONSTRUCTION is a 65-day course focusing more on the principles and techniques of management of underwater construction projects. Students learn how to estimate material, manpower, and equipment/resources and draft required correspondence. They also learn to supervise precision demolition operations, manage demolition resources, and execute emergency procedures.

SALVAGE/CONSTRUCTION DEMOLITION DIVER (SCDD) is a 20-day course designed to provide the knowledge and skills required to use military standard and precision special purpose munitions plus mechanical and chemical cutting equipment for salvage, battle damage repair, and underwater construction operations. Techniques and procedures for quick ingress and total ship sectioning during wrecking-in-place operations are included. The emphasis is on state of the art materials, equipment, and techniques.

DIVER FIRST CLASS (1C) is a 40-day course designed to provide qualified Second Class Divers with the advanced training necessary to not only perform operational air diving as a dive team member, but to better understand the responsibilities and duties of a diving supervisor. Instruction includes advanced diving physics and medicine, dive system certification, planning for all manner of surface-supplied diving operations, open-circuit scuba, and hyperbaric chamber operations.

MEDICAL DEEP SEA DIVING TECHNICIAN is a 119-day course designed to provide qualified Hospital Corpsmen (HM) with the training necessary to perform surface-supplied diving as a team member/diver and to understand the responsibilities and duties of a

Army Master Diver

diving supervisor. Instruction includes advanced diving physics, medicine, and underwater physiology to enable the hospital corpsman to understand the effects of pressure on the human body and the treatment of diving related injuries such as the bends (DCS) and gas embolisms (AGE). There is particular emphasis on this course in the use of Navy standard decompression tables and running decompression diving operations. The prerequisite is qualification as Hospital Corpsman, and since all US Navy Diving Medical Technicians (DMTs) are trained in all aspects of diving, the first 20 weeks is the same as the Diver Second Class training.

DIVER EXPLOSIVE ORDNANCE DISPOSAL is a 61-day course designed to provide qualified personnel with the basic training necessary to safely perform as an Explosive Ordnance Disposal (EOD) team member using scuba or MK-16 mixed-gas rebreather. This course provides training in diving physics, identifying diving injuries, and recognizing the need for treatment. Training evolutions include underwater searches, hull inspections, small boat seamanship, introduction to underwater electronic search equipment and mine counter-measures (MCM) operations.

EOD MIXED GAS DIVING UBA (MK-16) is a 10-day course which provides qualified personnel with the basic training required to maintain and perform diving operations using the MK-16 closed-circuit underwater breathing apparatus (UBA). The MK-16 is a diving system that is considerably more complex and requires more set-up and

YTD logo.

One hundred and thirty-one-foot YTD-17 Neptune.

NDSTC dockside and ascent tower.

NDSTC basic training pool.

Scuba divers practice problem-solving drills in the NDSTC pool.

maintenance than basic scuba. Instruction encompasses diving closed-circuit breathing apparatus, emergency procedures, various corrective maintenance, preventive maintenance, pre-dive and post-dive of the UBA, and instruction in the use of auxiliary equipment such as the gas transfer system (GTS).

HeO$_2$ DIVER is an unclassified 14-day course which provides qualified First Class divers follow-on training in all phases of surface supplied mixed-gas diving using heli-ox mixtures (HeO$_2$). Instruction includes extensive training in surface supplied mixed-gas diving, diving medicine, and operations of transfer/mixing equipment. Prerequisite courses are: U.S. Diver First Class, Diving Medical Technician, Basic Diving Officer, or Diving Medical Officer.

SATURATION DIVER is an 18-day course that provides the theory behind saturation diving for qualified First Class divers, medical deep sea diving technicians, deep sea (HeO$_2$) diving officers, and undersea medical officers. Instruction includes saturation diving theory and operation and maintenance of atmospheric monitoring equipment. Prerequisite courses are: US Diver First Class, Diving Medical Technician, Basic Diving Officer, or Diving Medical Officer.

USMC COMBATANT DIVER (MCD) is 35 training days in length. This physically demanding program with long ocean swims is divided into four modules of instruction: Physical Conditioning, Combat diver fundamentals, USMC Open-Circuit SCUBA, and USMC Closed-Circuit (MK25) operations. The course provides underwater infiltration tactical training in accordance with current Marine Corps training and mission performance standards.

AMPHIBIOUS RECONNAISSANCE CORPSMAN is a 15-day course to provide qualified SCUBA/LAR V Hospital Corpsman diver personnel (NEC 8403) with the basic training necessary to perform medical functions, duty as a recompression chamber supervisor and inside tender, dive team member/diver in SCUBA and LAR V (MK25) in support of USMC Reconnaissance operations.

MASTER DIVER (MDV) is a 10-day course which evaluates qualified First Class Divers and Saturation Divers, E-7 or above, to determine the candidates ability to successfully perform as Diving Supervisors in all facets of Navy Diving. This course is for evaluation purposes only and as such is not available for international students.

ARMY DIVER PROGRAMS

Since the Navy, through NDSTC and SUPDIVE, is the subject matter expert on diving for all branches of the US military, the Army conducts their engineering and diving programs at the school. Delta Company, 577th Engineer Battalion, operates three Army Engineer diving courses.

ENGINEER DIVER is 130 training days and teaches entry-level SCUBA and surface-supplied diving skills as well as army-specific tasks such as underwater mine and counter-mine operations, underwater demolitions, and engineer reconnaissance.

Dockside dive stations (left) and free ascent tower (FAT).

ENGINEER DIVER BASIC NON-COMMISSIONED OFFICER is a 70-day course of instruction that Staff Sergeants receive to become Army First Class Divers. Additionally, the soldiers receive engineer-specific training focusing on operations planning.

ARMY MASTER DIVER COURSE is the pinnacle of Army dive training. Successful completion of this 20-day course results in the award of the Master Diver Badge. The course includes classroom testing and training and a rigorous 3-day performance evaluation

COURSES FOR DIVING OFFICERS

BASIC DIVING OFFICER (BDO) is an 80-day course that provides students with the training necessary to perform operational air, surface supported, and scuba diving, and to possess the knowledge and duties of the Diving Officer. Instruction includes diving physics and medicine, underwater tools, salvage, diving system certification, scuba, and surface supported air diving operations, and diving related risk management and supervision. This course qualifies trainees to a depth of 190 feet.

SALVAGE DIVING OFFICER is a 31-day course that provides qualified diving officers follow-on training in all phases of salvage operations. Instruction includes salvage seamanship, salvage machinery, salvage computation, and practical experience in conducting and supervising salvage operations. Students complete their final phase of training by performing diving operations under actual at-sea conditions while raising a salvage hulk from the bottom of the harbor. Prerequisite course is Basic Diving Officer.

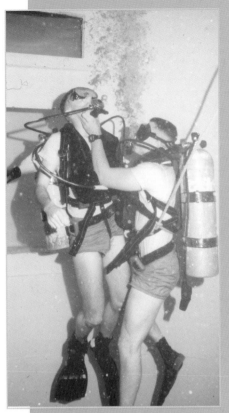

Unconscious diver rescue drills.

Scuba divers training in the 50-foot ascent tower.

Army Engineering Second Class Divers preparing to dive the ascent tower.

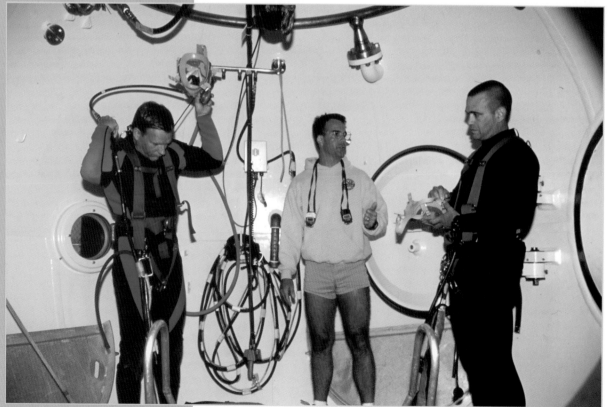

Divers with full face masks in the PVA.

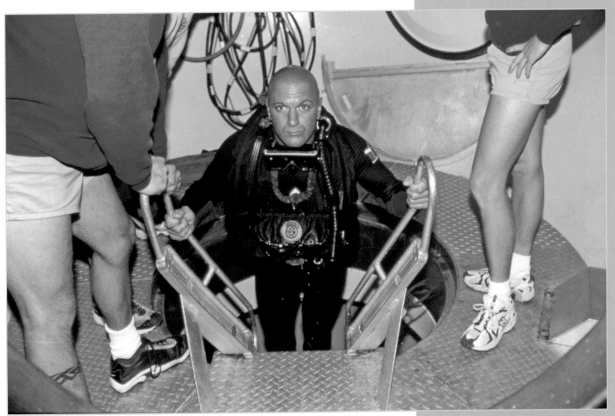

Diver exits the PVA wet pot.

Divers prepare for a 190-foot dive in the PVA wet pot.

PVA chamber and entry lock.

EOD divers prepare their MK16 mixed-gas rebreathers.

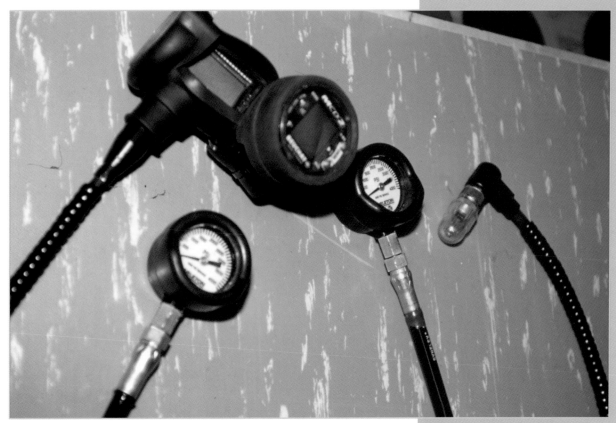

MK16 instrumentation.

The guts of an MK16. The large dome on left is the scrubber canister housing.

*EOD divers prepare for ocean
training.*

*Final bubble checks before going
sub-surface.*

*EOD divers prepare for
underwater sonar search.*

*Dockside surface supply and
scuba training at NDSTC.*

The giant stride entry.

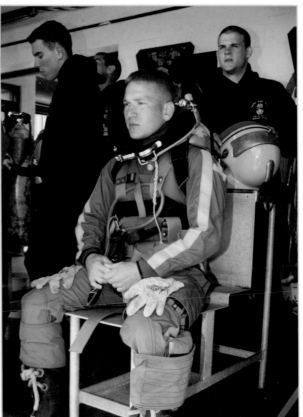

Stand-by diver.

MK21 training.

NDSTC instructor "Gold Shirt" MDV Brad Flemming.

Welding training in the NDSTC welding and burning tanks.

HYPERBARIC MEDICAL OFFICER (HMO); RECOGNITION & TREATMENT (R&T) OF DIVING CASUALTIES is a 10 day course designed to provide Medical Officers with the basic training necessary to safely and effectively perform as a medical advisor for hyperbaric treatments and to evaluate divers and diver candidates prior to diving.

MEDICAL DEPARTMENT DIVING OFFICER is a 45-day course designed to provide qualified medical officers with the training necessary to operate with the dive team as a consultant, team member, or diver during surface-supplied diving operations. Instruction includes hyperbaric physiology, surface supported deep sea diving systems, air, scuba, and lightweight diving systems. This course is designed as part of the six-month Naval Undersea Medical Institute course which qualifies trainees as Medical Department Diving Officers. Prerequisite course is Medical Officer Undersea International taught at the Naval Undersea Medical Institute in Groton, Connecticut.

DIVING MEDICAL OFFICER (DMO) is a nine-week course designed for Undersea Medical Officer Candidates to complete their six months of instruction in Undersea Medicine. This course is essentially the R&T course with an extra week of advanced lectures and laboratory, coupled with six weeks of dive training. On completion of this course graduates are certified US Navy Divers. Students are certified or familiarized on every diving system in use today in the military. Unlike the R&T course, physical training is mandatory and intense. Many students are dropped from training due to inability to keep up with PT.

Graduates of this course are NOT authorized to wear the Navy UMO pin. To qualify for this, candidates must complete the entire six-month Undersea Medical Officer Course offered at the Naval Undersea Medical Institute.

Welding and burning training during 2C dive program.

*NDSTC welding training tank
diver prepares to strike an arc.*

Ready to weld.

EOD diving officer.

*NDSTC Engineering Officer LT
Carolyn Wisner (2001).*

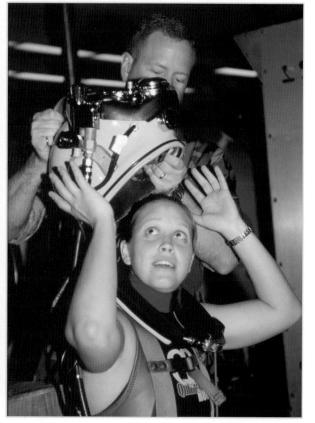

US Marine combat divers at NDSTC.

Diving the Drager MK25 CCBA.

MK25 shallow water rebreather.

*MCD rebreather dive lab
and classroom.*

Pre-dive checks.

Pre-breathing oxygen.

Assembling the MK25.

Recon Marines with MK25 and BDUs over their wetsuits.

Pre-breathing oxygen and purging the rebreather.

Platoon of recon divers moving out for a 2000-meter training swim.

Underwater Ship & Submarine Husbandry

usbandry is the Navy's term for maintenance and repair of their ships and submarines extending below the waterline through the use of divers to avoid the prohibitive costs and inconvenience of dry-docking. In addition to basic hull repair and screw changes, the simple cleaning of marine growth from the hull of a large ship can not only increase the ship's speed but also save millions of dollars in fuel costs.

Teams of Navy divers are stationed at most major Naval bases to carry out the essential underwater husbandry tasks that, in addition to screw changes and hull cleaning, can include the replacement and repair of zinc corrosion protection systems, underwater inspection and photography, underwater welding, sonar dome repair, replacement of auxiliary propulsion units, water intake inspection and cleaning, and drilling into bearings to inspect with a bore-scope.

Changing a screw on a large battleship or aircraft carrier is no easy job. Apart from the fact that the propellers can be over 21 feet in diameter and top the scales at 40 tons, the divers must break them loose with mechanical and hydraulic tools in the near-zero visibility waters of a port or harbor.

The largest ship's husbandry dive teams are the Consolidated Divers Unit in San Diego, Ships Intermediate Maintenance in Norfolk, and the Regional Shipyard Dive Locker in Washington.

There are also submarine husbandry dive teams in San Diego, Bangor, Washington, and Groton, Connecticut. In addition to the Navy divers assigned to ship and sub husbandry, the Navy also contracts diving and underwater welding services from civilian diving contractors such as Phoenix and Puget Sound Divers.

The following excerpt from Captain Chris Murray's article titled The Navy Dive Team[1] does an excellent job of describing husbandry divers. "UWSH divers usually spend more of their time working underwater than do their counterparts assigned to sea duty as they complete the repairs needed to allow ships to get underway to meet tight deployment commitments. The skills they develop in becoming experienced experts also are helpful in preparing them for wartime missions. A seasoned UWSH diver is a valuable asset in carrying out combat salvage missions.

"Navy divers completed extraordinary ship-husbandry feats underwater when they replaced two propellers on the nuclear-powered aircraft carrier USS *John C. Stennis* in August, 1999. Divers from Consolidated Divers Unit (CDU) San Diego, Calif., and Puget Sound Naval Shipyard (PSNS), Wash., safely coordinated the removal and replacement of the 63,000-pound propellers at Naval Air Station North Island, Calif. A combined crew of 16 Navy divers, six civilian shipyard divers, and a NAVSEA diver/engineer worked side by side both on the surface and in the water—12 hours a day for 20 days. Two dive stations, loaded with tools and other equipment items that were neither lightweight nor very portable, were used periodically to support up to five surface-supplied divers in the water at one time."

CDU Distrubutor

CDU Lock. RCF 6,500 recompression facility.

CDU operator.

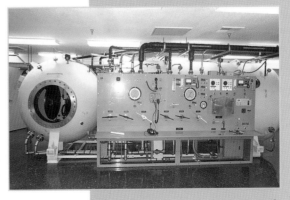

CDU panel.

*CDU divers working on the
rudder of the USS* Constellation.

*"The Connie" in port at North
Island Naval Station.*

CDU diver brief.

Time to work.

Chief diver Steve Strange, British
Royal Navy attached to CDU.

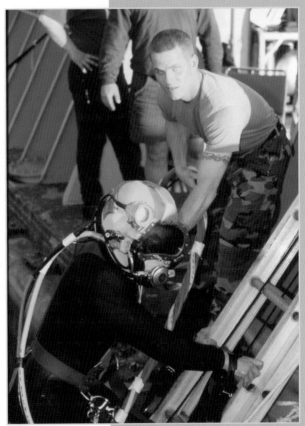

CDU diver tendered by
diver Dave Rehl.

CONSOLIDATED DIVERS UNIT (CDU)

Based out of the Naval Station 32nd Street in San Diego, CDU is the primary ship's husbandry diving asset for the southwestern region. The fifty-five Navy divers working out of CDU are responsible for a broad range of sub-surface ships maintenance, cleaning, and repair. CDU also supports a diving Detachment at the submarine base at Point Loma to handle submarine husbandry.

CDU was born out of a pilot program, created in 1979, to consolidate the Navy divers in San Diego to determine if this would more efficiently utilize diving assets and create cost savings to the fleet. The first year of the program was a success, so in August, 1980, the diving unit was officially commissioned as Harbor Clearance Unit One Detachment. The Unit's name was later changed to Mobile Diving & Salvage Unit One Detachment — MDSU-1 Det (pronounced "mud-sue").

This consolidation created several benefits to the Navy, doubling both the number of dives and bottom times with no increase in personnel. This was also the nexus of a West Coast based hull-cleaning program that saved the Navy $80 million annually in fuel costs. Ships with marine growth on the hull are slower and burn more fuel, and over extended at-sea deployments this has significance, both fiscally and tactically.

Stand-by diver Mike Wiltshire.

CDU diver Hoover with CO CMDR Kelly Eley in background.

Mobile UWSH diving control van.

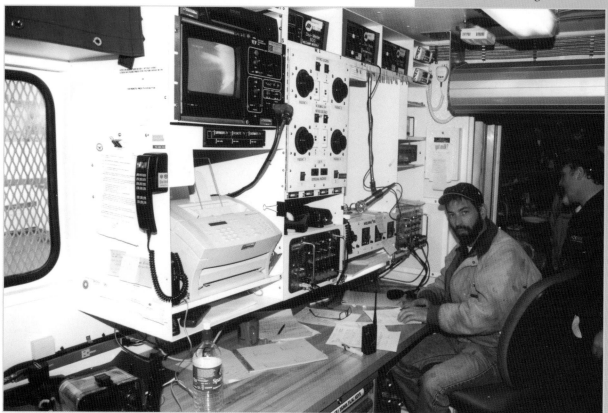

Interior of the UWSH diving and welding control van.

*Former CDU Executive Officer
CWO4 Rick Armstrong (2001).*

*Diver drilling into
the broken keyway.*

*Changing drill bits under the
USS* Constellation.

MK21 diver CWO4 Armstrong with digital camera.

Author returns from photographing CDU divers at work under the aircaft carrier USS Constellation *(2001).*

In-water decompression.

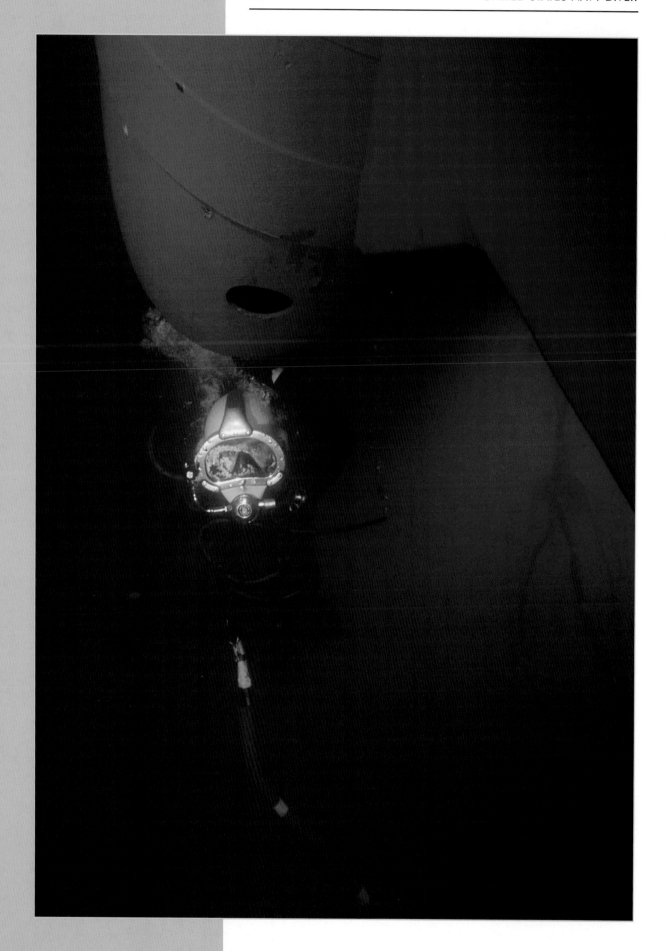

The combination of manpower and technical expertise at MDSU-1 Det resulted in the development of special underwater work procedures for a number of jobs and classes of ships, including underwater screw changes and the change-out of controllable reversible pitch (CRP) blades. The Det also established a central database for underwater work and hull cleaning performed on the Pacific Fleet and West Coast based ships.

MDSU-1 Det salvage personnel maintained the only West Coast Fly-Away Diving System (FADS) with complete salvage capability. They successfully salvaged a number of ship's anchors, crashed aircraft, and grounded ships, saving the Navy an estimated $100 million dollars. In addition, they conducted training aimed at the certification of the Navy's first underwater welders.

MK21 diver with welding visor.

In October 1986, MDSU-1 Det was re-designated as Consolidated Divers Unit (CDU). The command's primary focus became underwater ship's husbandry with the salvage aspects of the command's mission being transferred to Mobile Diving & Salvage Unit One in Hawaii.

As of 2001, CDU was functioning smoothly under the supervision of Commander Richard Kelly Eley, CWO4 Armstrong, Command Master Chief (MDV) "Brick" Bradford, and Master Diver Chief Bob Barker.

SHORE INTERMEDIATE MAINTENANCE ACTIVITY (SIMA)

Located in the heart of the US Atlantic Fleet in Norfolk, Virginia, the SIMA can boast the largest dive locker in the United States Navy. The dive locker has 75 military billets and employs 29 DOD civilian divers dedicated to providing Underwater Ship's Husbandry (UWSH) for both surface ships and submarines in the Mid-Atlantic region.

Over the years, several Master Divers and Chiefs have left their mark on the SIMA dive locker, making it the superb operation it is today. These have included MVD Tom Stock, MVD Jeff Royce, MDV Frank Perna, MDV John Spires, MDV Douglas Roberson, and Diving Officer Chief Warrant Officer Mikulski.

SIMA divers are deployed in three military dive teams designated A, B & C, with 14 Navy divers and a Master Diver per team. There are also two teams of civilian divers working at SIMA, designated D & E with 10–15 divers per team.

The primary dive platforms for these teams are five 50-foot dive boats set-up for surface-supply diving and two vehicles, including a $750,000 Dive & Drive mobile dive station. This impressive dive truck on steroids is fully equipped to support three surface supplied divers and all the required support equipment.

CDU diving support platform
at Point Loma.

CDU diver in MK20 FFM.

Nuclear submarine at Point Loma sub base, California.

In addition to an 8,000 square foot waterfront building, SIMA has a 3,000 square foot hyperbaric facility. The types of jobs that SIMA divers tackle on a daily basis include cofferdams, inspections, propeller changes, and auxiliary propulsion motor replacements. They are rightfully proud of the occasional big jobs, such as a 40-ton propeller replacement done at the Philadelphia Naval Shipyard—which is summed up in the command's simple motto, "We Fix Ships, Underwater."

INTERMEDIATE MAINTENANCE FACILITY (IMF)

Another significant ship's husbandry operation within CONUS is the Intermediate Maintenance Facility in Bangor, Washington. This maintenance facility, along with others in the Northwest, is supported by the Regional Shipyard Dive Locker and overseen by a Navy Master Diver. The Navy also utilizes civilian divers, many of them former Navy divers, on some projects, including the Bremerton Ship Yard diving operations.

The US Navy also maintains shipyards in Hawaii and Japan to service the Pacific Fleet. At the Pearl Harbor Shipyard and Intermediate Maintenance Facility ship's husbandry diving is handled by divers from Mobile Diving & Salvage Unit ONE (MDSU-1) Fleet Maintenance Dive Department stationed right next door. At the US Navy Ship Repair Facility (SRF) in Yokosuka, Japan, diving operations are handled by Japanese civilian divers trained and supervised by the US Navy.

*CDU divers equipped
with MK20 FFM.*

SUBMARINE HUSBANDRY

In addition to ship's maintenance, Navy divers are also required to service a significantly large fleet of nuclear submarines. This type of specialized husbandry is undertaken at the submarine bases located at Point Loma, San Diego; Bangor, Washington; Norfolk, Virginia; and Groton, Connecticut.

Submarine husbandry divers perform a wide variety of maintenance functions for the submarine fleet, including rope guard inspections, screw changes, running gear inspections, stave bearing inspection and replacements, hull and mud tank inspections, external hatch inspections, and counter measures pod removal and replacement.

Because of the restricted external access to a submarine's hull and the tight workspace within these spaces, the Navy divers will utilize the MK 20 Aga mask with a lightweight umbilical.

Before any work can begin on the outside of the submarine, there is a lengthy shutdown procedure needed to ensure the safety of the divers. This requires close coordination between the submarine's crew and the dive team supervisor, along with "red-tagging" of any valves or controls that may endanger the divers.

MK20 is used to access the sub's ballast tanks and restricted spaces.

MUD PUPPY PROGRAMS

As with other commands such as MDSU2 and EOD, CDU operates a Mud Puppy program for sailors possessing a sincere interest in becoming Navy divers. The Mud Puppy program is designed to prepare prospective candidates for the rigors of Navy Dive School, both physically and academically. This mentoring program reduces the washout rate at the dive school by giving candidates the training and confidence to take on the challenges of Navy diving.

Candidates interested in participating in this program are screened prior to submitting a package for dive school. The screening process begins at their command, and includes a diving physical with a chest x-ray, an interview with a Master Diver or Diving Officer, the Divers PT Test, and a pressure test to 60 fsw in a hyperbaric facility.

Candidates that successfully complete all these requirements can then submit their package for school and go to a diving command that offers the Mud Puppy Program. CDU takes great pride in preparing sailors for dive school, so the program at CDU encompasses four basic areas of training that will greatly enhance the candidate's ability to successfully complete Diver Second Class training. (1) Extensive physical fitness training to include aerobic and strength conditioning through running, swimming, and calisthenics; (2) Academic training through an interactive computer self-paced diving medicine and physics course that must be successfully completed prior to attending dive school; (3) Real time diving operational experience by being involved in actual underwater ship's husbandry repairs as topside tenders and acting in various capacities to assist in underwater ship's repair; (4) Developing the CONFIDENCE to attend Second Class Diver Training at NDSTC and be SUCCESSFUL[2].

NOTE: By the time this book goes to print, CDU and SIMA will have undergone a name change. CDU will be South West Regional Maintenance Center Divers (RMC Divers), and SIMA will be Mid-Atlantic Regional Maintenance Center Divers.

ENDNOTES

1   The Navy Dive Team - Making the Impossible Look Easy - By Christopher C. Murray and Michael P. Leese. Capt. Christopher C. Murray, USN, is the Navy's supervisor of diving at the Naval Sea Systems Command (NAVSEA). Michael P. Leese is a diving project engineer at NAVSEA.

2   CDU command web page.

Mobile Diving &
Salvage Unit One

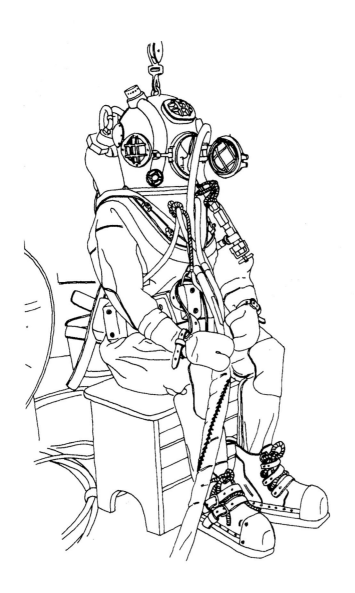

8

"WHERE PRIDE & PROFESSIONALISM RUN DEEP"

Salvage divers are a unique breed, always looking for their next big operation and pushing for an opportunity to dive. While fleet maintenance divers and underwater construction teams (UCT) dive almost everyday, divers assigned to salvage units and salvage ships do not get the regular diving opportunities of their shore-side brethren. But when the call does come, it is usually in the wake of some disaster such as an aircraft crashing at sea, and the divers know the diving will be both challenging and dangerous.

In fact, there is no maritime occupation more dangerous than salvage work, not just because of the unpredictable nature of the sea, but because the salvage itself is usually the result of some horrific event. Salvage divers must contend with not only rough seas, dark waters, and dangerous currents, they must also negotiate the twisted wreckage, razor sharp metal, miles of broken tubing, and entangling cable and wire that are problematic on all crash sites.

When ships, planes, or helicopters go down in the ocean, or terrorists strike at sea, then it is the divers of the Mobile Diving & Salvage Units— MDSU (pronounced "mud sue") that get the urgent call. Maintaining a high level of readiness, MDSU commands are strategically located on the Atlantic seaboard in Little Creek, Virginia, and in the Pacific at Pearl Harbor. Each command also supports mobile detachments in the Mediterranean and San Diego.

The MDSU divers are heavily supported on operations by the Navy's purpose-built rescue and salvage ships — USS *Grasp* (ARS-51), USS *Grapple* (ARS-53), and USS *Salvor* (ARS-52) — all of which carry a full complement of divers, diving equipment, underwater tools, lifting capability, and recompression chambers.

MOBILE DIVING & SALVAGE UNIT ONE

Mission Statement: To provide swift and mobile ship salvage, towing, battle damage repair, deep ocean recovery, harbor clearance, and underwater ship repair capabilities in support of the Third and Seventh Fleets (Pacific Command).

Mobile Diving & Salvage Unit ONE (MDSU-1) was commissioned as Harbor Clearance Unit ONE in February 1966 in Subic Bay, Republic of the Philippines. The command was immediately put to the test in Vietnam, where salvage teams conducted numerous harbor clearance operations in Vietnamese rivers, harbors, and coastal areas. The unit's professionalism resulted in the command being awarded the Meritorious Unit Commendation and Navy Unit Citation, and at the conclusion of the Vietnam conflict the command was relocated to Pearl Harbor, Hawaii.

Continued on pg 110

Topside supervisor checks video feed from diver.

Fleet Maintenance Dive Department (FMDD) support platform.

FMDD dive console.

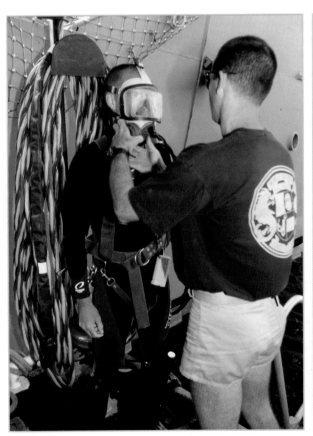

FMDD divers on surface-supplied MK20 FFM.

U.S. Navy nuclear submarine surfacing.

Salvage ship on a five point mooring with buoyancy tanks.

In 1979 the unit's mission was expanded to include responsibility for providing diving services to all Pearl Harbor-based surface ships; then in January 1982 the unit's name was changed from Harbor Clearance Unit ONE to Mobile Diving and Salvage Unit ONE to better reflect the capabilities of the unit. In 1996 the MDSU-1 mission was further expanded with the consolidation of the SUBASE dive locker into MDSU-1's Fleet Maintenance Dive Department (FMDD), making MDSU-1 responsible for providing all ship's husbandry diving services for watercraft, surface ships, and submarines in Pearl Harbor. (Note: FMDD has since separated from MDSU-1 and is now at Pearl Harbor Naval Shipyard.)

MDSU-1 uses a diverse range of specialized diving and recompression chamber systems to accomplish its mission, including a mixed-gas diving system capable of supporting dives to a depth of 300 feet. The unit's equipment is air transportable, giving MDSU-1 the ability to respond to diving and salvage missions anywhere within CINCPACFLT area of responsibility. MDSU-1 also supports four diving detachments — Det One, Three, Five, and Seven.

MDSU-1 area of responsibility is the entire Pacific, so their missions run the full gamut of ocean salvage, from ships running aground to aircraft down. Back in 1988 they recovered a helicopter in the Philippines using HeO_2 and an open bell at a depth greater than 200 fsw. In 2001 Det Five sent eight divers to Vietnam for 30 days to check on witness reports and dive the wreckage of Vietnamese Naval Coastal Patrol Boats. MDSU-1 also supported MDSU-2 with divers on the *Monitor* project and several other major operations.

USS *SALVOR* (ARS 52)

Just as USS *Grasp* and USS *Grapple* support East Coast operations, the USS *Salvor* supports the Pacific Fleet and MDSU-1. At a length of 255 feet and a beam of 51 feet, the Auxiliary Rescue Salvage (ARS) design ships are ideally suited to salvage work.

Based out of Pearl Harbor, the USS *Salvor* is mission built for salvage, rescue, towing, and underwater recovery, and comes fully equipped for manned diving operations. With a steel double-lock chamber and 190-foot air diving capability, the *Salvor* carries all the underwater tools and lifting equipment necessary for salvage. Diving equipment is primarily MK21 surface-supplied diving systems and SCUBA gear. The *Salvor* can also support Deep Drone, the Navy's 7,200-foot depth rated salvage ROV.

The full complement of crew is 6 officers and 84 enlisted; of those the dive team is usually made up of 2 Diving Officers, a Master Diver and 14 enlisted divers. As much as they would prefer to be diving all the time, all ship's divers pull double duty in crew positions when not in diving mode.

USS Salvor *in home port at Pearl Harbor, Hawaii.*

EHIME MARU RECOVERY
OPERATION

In early 2001, the command staff and divers at MDSU-1 unexpectedly found themselves with a major salvage and recovery operation right in their own front yard. At approximately 1:50pm (HST), 9 February, the nuclear submarine USS *Greeneville* (SSN 772) collided with a Japanese fishing ship while attempting an emergency main ballast tank blow procedure south of Diamond Head, off Honolulu, Hawaii.

Responding to the accident in rescue mode, the US Coast Guard was able to rescue twenty-six survivors, but tragically nine souls went down with the ship in deep water and were declared missing. The US Navy immediately launched a major operation to locate the missing victims and ship, and as a sign of goodwill, pledged to try and recover the victims if technically possible.

The Commander in Chief, Pacific Fleet (CINCPACFLT) called on the Supervisor of Salvage and Diving (SUPSALV), and Submarine Development Squadron 5 (SUBDEVRON 5) from San Diego, to mobilize their ROVs for the subsurface search. SUPSALV deployed the ROV Deep Drone and the Shallow Water Intermediate Search System (SWISS) side scanning sonar, and DEVRON 5 deployed the ROV Scorpio[1].

On Friday, February 16, the Navy found *Ehime Maru* sitting nearly upright in 2,003 feet of water, approximately 1,000 yards from the collision site reported by USS *Greeneville*. The remotely operated vehicle (ROV) Scorpio II detected *Ehime Maru* with its onboard sonar at 11:25 pm.

Then positive identification was confirmed at 11:29 pm by reading the vessel's stern plate with the aid of Scorpio's video camera and powerful lights. After the vessel was identified, a visual search of the exterior and surrounding seafloor was made, but no victims were located.

What followed was to become one of the most challenging deep-water recoveries in Navy diving history. Since divers could not work at two thousand feet, the Navy would need to raise the ship and move it to shallower waters for the divers to begin search and recovery operations. To do this, the salvage engineers devised an elaborate recovery system using an oilfield drilling and diving support ship, *Rockwater 2*, supported on the bottom by ROVs. Once lifted from the seabed, the *Ehime Maru* would be carefully moved to shallower waters, where Navy divers would be able to drop down and search the vessel for the nine missing crewmembers.

The proposed dive team would be made up of US Navy divers and Japanese divers from the U.S. Navy Ship Repair Facility (SRF), Yokosuka, Japan, with participation by the Japan Maritime Self-Defense Force divers for final inspection before the ship was moved back to deeper waters.

Overall Command of this politically and culturally sensitive diving operation fell squarely in the lap of MDSU ONE CO Commander Robert Fink, his XO LCDR Ron "Leith" Parslow, Operations Officer LCDR George Byford, and Command Master Chief MMCM (DSW/MDV) Jim Nichols. The Officer-in-Charge of diving for the *Ehime Maru* project was Chief Warrant Officer George Primavera.

The recovery of the *Ehime Maru* was to be a humanitarian mission unlike anything these officers and divers had dealt with before. It was not a classified mission, but as Commander Fink described it, "this mission had a degree of sensitivity beyond aircraft recovery. It had to be sensitive to Japanese custom."

Briefing for the Ehime Maru
recovery (2001).

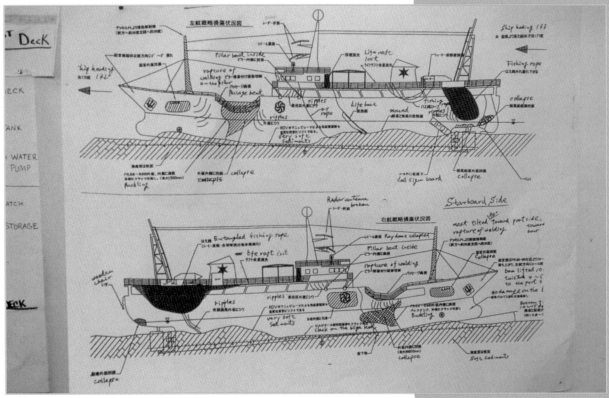

Plans of the Ehime Maru
showing damage and debris.

*MDSU-1 and attached divers
training for EM recovery (2001).*

Commander Robert Fink.

Chief Warrant Officer Primavera.

*EM recovery divers worked in
two teams—Blue and Gold.*

*Japanese divers from the U.S. Navy
Ship Repair facility (SRF)
in Yokosuka.*

MK21 diver with Viking drysuit.

MDSU-1 divers and command personnel would lead the diving effort, but because of the projected size and duration of this recovery effort, additional US Navy deep-sea and EOD divers were brought in from a number of commands to assist on the operation.

After considerable planning, and as salvage engineers wrestled with the problem of lifting the *Ehime Maru* from deep water, spin-ups for the diving phase of the operation got underway on the 6th of August.[2] With over fifty divers and support personnel assembled for the initial training evolutions, command personnel and engineers gave a detailed brief on the proposed operation. Of greatest interest to the divers was the layout of the *Ehime Maru*: access hatches, companionways, cabins, galley, and engineering areas, all of which the divers would have to negotiate in the search for the missing victims.

The divers were also given detailed information as to where the victims were last seen at the time of the collision. One was last seen in the pilothouse, three in the students' mess, and possibly three more crewmembers in the engine room.

Immediately after the briefing, training began in earnest dockside at the MDSU-1 command. The divers and diving supervisors focused their initial training on mastering drysuit diving procedures, diver decontamination, and efficiently stripping the diver down for surface decompression in the portable deck chambers.

Dock-side training at MDSU-1.

*MDV Doug Wesling (far left)
with* Ehime Maru *recovery
dive team "Gold."*

Giant stride entry off the dock.

MDV Fred Orns.

Stand-by diver.

Drysuit training.

MK 21 lights and video.

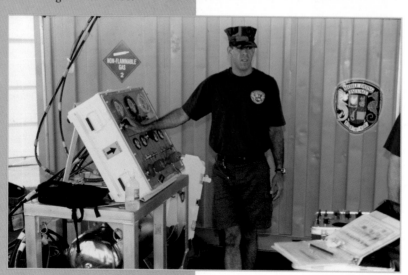

MK III diving control system.

The command had opted to train with Viking drysuits because of the potential for contamination from the ship's fuel oils (approximately 45,000 gallons of marine diesel), and large stocks of rotting fish in the holds.

The divers were divided into two teams, Blue and Gold, with 25–27 divers on each team and with the Japanese SRF divers integrated into both teams. Since the Japanese divers were already US Navy trained and familiar with the MK 21, it was just a matter of getting them comfortable in the Viking drysuits and the post-dive procedures for diver decontamination and decompression.

Also there to support the recovery were the divers from the USS *Salvor* under the watchful eye of Master Diver BMCS (SW/MDV) Fred Orns.

Training and preparations for the recovery continued in an efficient and professional manner, pausing only on 11 September when the United States came under attack by terrorist hijackers.

Ready to dive.

*Climbing out with over
100 lbs of gear.*

*Viking dry suit training
under the pier.*

Diver decontamination.

Decontamination and scrub down.

After removing the mast with shaped cutting charges, the salvage engineers, with more than their share of headaches, were able to raise the *Ehime Maru,* and on 14 October, following a long, slow, 13-mile journey, the fishing ship was set down in 110 feet (33m) of water off Reef Runway near Pearl Harbor[3].

After a 24-hour period to allow the ship to settle, the first team of Navy SCUBA divers conducted an external inspection and video to verify that hatches still gave access to the ship's interior. The second team rigged lines, set ladders, and placed inclinometers on the vessel to monitor the ship's stability. It was planned that a third team would check the bridge for victims last seen in the pilothouse.

To handle the number of personnel required for the operation, and to facilitate diving operations, the Navy divers deployed from a 400-foot work and accommodation barge hired from Crowley Marine services. This was anchored over the dive site with a six-point mooring system.

The operational plan called for 70 divers divided into two separate dive stations, working 16 hours a day for 33 days. Divers were drawn from the three MDSU Detachments, SRF Yokosuka, EOD Units THREE and ELEVEN, the Submarine Training Center Pacific, the Dive School and submarine rescue ship USS *Salvor.* If you were a Navy diver at this time, this was the operation to be on, and divers from all over the fleet wanted in.

After it was established that the *Ehime Maru* was not going to roll unexpectedly, surface-supplied diving began in earnest. Penetration into the ship had to proceed with caution as bulkheads and overheads had sustained severe damage, leaving passageways on all four decks blocked with wreckage. There were also the hazards of other debris, fishnets, some 4000 fishhooks, bait, fuel, jammed doors, and sharp edges caused by implosions.

The first dive teams, working in MK21s with lights and video cameras, had the difficult task of debris removal before teammates could penetrate deeper into the wreck. The plan was to clear two compartments per day with five dives.

The divers' primary mission objective was to find and recover the missing crewmembers, with a secondary task of recovering their personal effects for the families. The third objective was met when divers recovered unique shipboard items that could be used for a memorial, such as the ship's bell, helm controls, shrine, nameplate, ensign, and anchors. All of this work was recorded by the diver's helmet mounted video for the Japanese government and family members.

The forth mission objective was the most challenging — to remove hazardous liquids and materials from the *Ehime Maru.* To remove the fuels and oils that had escaped from the ruptured tanks and were trapped in the overheads, divers used suction wands, but accessing the

Going operational.

diesel in the fuel tanks required "hot tap" techniques. These placed valves into the side of the tanks, allowing the fuel to be removed by hose to the surface. To complete this mission objective, divers also removed other materials from the wreck that posed a hazard to the environment or marine life. This included over 100,000 meters of fishing long-line and an estimated two tons of debris.

The fifth and final task for the divers was to rig the lifting assembly to move the *Ehime Maru* to its final resting place. The divers rigged lifting plates and a spreader bar suspended from the contractor barge, followed by exothermic cutting devices attached on the lift wires.

The ship was lifted by ballasting-down the barge and then de-ballasting after the lifting chains and cables were attached. *Ehime Maru* was then towed back to sea and laid to rest in 8500 feet of water on 25 November, 2001.

In 33 days of diving, MDSU-ONE logged over 650 dives and 625 hours of bottom time without diver mishap to complete a task of complexity not seen since Pearl Harbor salvage efforts in the late forties. Between 15 October and 6 November, Navy divers successfully recovered the bodies of eight of the nine missing crewmembers, and Japanese military divers also made 101 dives, but were unable to find the final missing victim.

To quote CWO3 Primavera — "This is a testimony to the pride and professionalism of the Navy Divers."[3]

Quoting the Deputy Chief Cabinet Secretary of Japan, "The *Ehime Maru* accident was a regrettable incident, but the U.S. Navy overcame numerous difficulties and dangers, and despite the terrorist attacks on the U.S. Mainland, completed the unprecedented and difficult operation of lifting the *Ehime Maru* and then put all its efforts in completing the search and recovery operations."

ENDNOTES

1. "Behind the Scenes with the US Navy: Recovering the Ehime Maru" By LCDR Greg Baumann, Faceplate July/August 2002.
2. Author was invited to observe the spin-ups August, 2001.
3. Edited from an article by CWO3 George Primavera, Faceplate March, 2002.

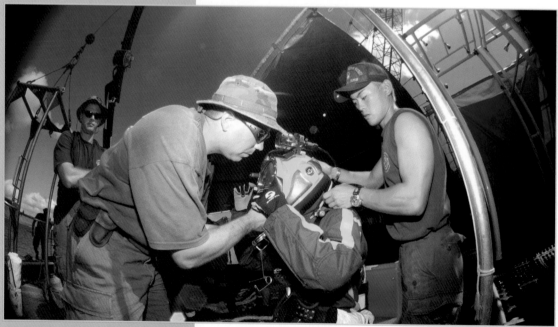

Preparing for dives on the Ehime Maru.

Supporting the weight of the helmet for the diver.

Diver tenders.

Diver Supervisor Irvin Connelly.

Focused and ready to dive.

Descending to the Ehime Maru.

On the Ehime Maru.

Initial inspection divers.

Scuba survey.

Recovering the divers—shadow of the work barge is seen above the diver.

Mobile Diving & Salvage Unit Two

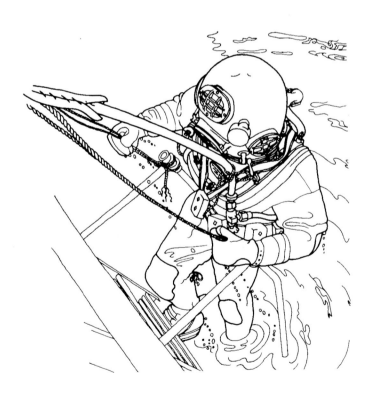

9

"PRIDE, PROFESSIONALISM, TEAMWORK"

*M*obile Diving and Salvage Unit TWO, located at Naval Amphibious Base (NAB) Little Creek, was originally established as Harbor Clearance Unit TWO on 01 October 1966. Patterned after World War II mobile salvage units, MDSU-2 consolidated the diving resources of the Atlantic Fleet in order to clear harbors and waterways during the Vietnam War[1].

The command officially became Mobile Diving and Salvage Unit TWO in February of 1982, reflecting the new focus on salvage operations and specialized diving missions. Over the years, MDSU-2 earned the title of "Experts in Salvage" through participation in such unique operations as the recovery of TWA Flight 800 (1996), Swiss Air Flight 111 (1998), JFK Jr's plane (1999), re-floating of YFU-83 in Puerto Rico, response to the USS *Cole*, the salvage of the USS *Monitor*, and recovery of Haitian ferry victims.

Recently, the heavy salvage capabilities of MDSU-2 were demonstrated during the salvage of the Titan IV spacecraft off the coast of Cape Canaveral. The global reach of mobile salvage diving also allows for quick response to demanding and emergent taskings such as the recovery of a SH-60 helicopter in 270 feet of water in the Red Sea.

USS *GRASP* & USS *GRAPPLE*

Even though MDSU-2 has earned the title "Experts in Salvage," few operations are undertaken on the eastern seaboard without the support of the Auxiliary Rescue Salvage (ARS) vessels USS *Grasp* (ARS-51) and USS *Grapple* (ARS-53). Both these hard working "junk boats" come with a complement of 6 officers and approximately 95 enlisted—including Diving Officers, Master Divers, and at least 14 divers on each.

Command headquarters.

USS Grasp *ARS-51.*

At 255 feet, powered by four Caterpillar diesel engines, both salvage ships come with a 40-ton aft boom for recovery work plus smaller diving davits. Not to neglect their wartime role, *Grasp* sports two 50-caliber machinegun weapons mounts while *Grapple* brings two MK-38 25mm chain guns to the fight.

The MK 21 air diving systems on both ships provide the salvage divers with the capability of tethered diving to 190 feet. The divers can descend to depth on a diving stage or in an open bell lowered by one of the two diving davits. For shallow underwater inspections, searches, and other tasks that require more mobility, the divers have the option of SCUBA. The onboard recompression chambers are used for treatment of divers suffering from decompression sickness, or for routine surface decompression, and are designed to mate with a portable recompression chamber at the outer lock entry door.[2]

USS *Grasp* and USS *Grapple* have both played pivotal roles in a number of high profile air crashes off the east coast, including the crash of Swiss Air 111, Egypt Air 990, JFK Jr.'s small plane, but none more challenging than the crash of TWA Flight 800 in 1996.

USS Grapple *ARS-53.*

TWA RECOVERY OPERATIONS

One of the largest operations for MDSU-2, USS *Grasp*, and USS *Grapple*, and one that brought modern Navy diving in to the nation's living rooms on the nightly news, was the crash and subsequent recovery of TWA Flight 800 in 1996. The following text, edited from an article by the Supervisor of Salvage & Diving during the operation, Captain Chip McCord,[3] best illustrates the scope and magnitude of this diving operation.

On 17 July at 20:32, TWA Flight 800, a Boeing 747 en route from New York's JFK airport to Paris, disappeared from radar contact. Eyewitnesses reported two explosions and a fire on the surface of the ocean.

The day after the crash the National Transportation Safety Board (NTSB) contacted the office of the Supervisor of Salvage (SUPSALV) and requested Navy assistance in recovering the cockpit voice recorder (CVR), the flight data recorder (FDR), commonly referred to as the "black box," and mapping the debris on the ocean bottom. However, the scope of Navy involvement was quickly expanded to encompass recovering the victims and the entire aircraft, to allow investigators to determine the cause of the crash.

USS Grapple, *2001. CPO Hardgraves returns from a 240-foot dive.*

Because the plane had crashed in relatively shallow water (120 feet), SUBSALV requested the support of Navy divers. EOD and Mobile Diving & Salvage initially provided 13 divers, support personnel, and the necessary equipment to establish a small command and control group and a Fly-Away Dive Locker (FADL) at a near-by Coast Guard station.

SUPSALV then came up with a three-phased approach to the operation—the first being the search and mapping phase. SUPSALV mobilized its ocean search and recovery contractor to lease a vessel (M/V *Pirouette*) with which to operate SUPSALV's side-scan sonar, towed pinger locator (to listen for the CVR and FDR pingers), and a miniature remotely operated vehicle (ROV) with video camera, sonar, and a robotic arm.

Recovering the divers.

By 19 July *Pirouette* was on scene and searching. The in-flight explosion of TWA 800 had broken the aircraft in two large pieces. The forward section of the fuselage was found about 1.5 miles from the aft section, and the entire aircraft debris field covered an area 4 miles long and 2 miles wide on the ocean floor. By the time the FDR had been found on 23 July, the recovery of victims had already been underway for three days.

Once the debris was found and mapped, the second phase of the operation was to recover the victims. This was done primarily by surface-supplied divers working from USS *Grasp* and USS *Grapple*, and with scuba divers working from small boats. The scuba diving operations were undertaken by Navy divers from over 20 commands, along with civilian divers from the NY State Police, NY City Police, Suffolk County Police, NY City Fire Department and the FBI. All diving operations were directed and coordinated by the Navy.

To help the divers in looking through the wreckage, SUPSALV mobilized three ROVs operated by Oceaneering, one each on *Grasp*, *Grapple* and *Pirouette*. The ROVs would log a total of 2641 hours on the bottom as the divers successfully recovered 109 victims. By the end of operations 216 of the 230 victims had been recovered.

The third and most grueling phase of the operation was to recover the aircraft wreckage needed to help investigators determine the cause of the crash. Wreckage recovery was actually started during the victim recovery phase, as it was often necessary to lift large pieces of wreckage to search under for victims. The decision was made to just bring the wreckage to the surface after the divers had hooked it up, rather than lifting the wreckage and then putting it back on the bottom.

To recover the wreckage, the large pieces were rigged by surface-supplied divers and lifted by the 40-ton booms from the *Grasp* and *Grapple*. The more mobile SCUBA divers located the scattered debris using portable GPS navigation and handheld sonars, similar to those used by EOD divers in mine detection. Recovery was made with a Navy Side Loading Warping Tug with a 10- to12-ton lift capability.

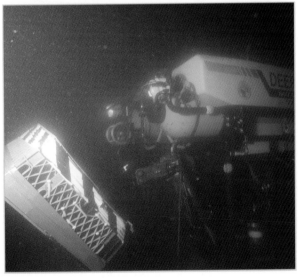

SUPSALV deep ROV working on TWA 800 recovery operations (August 1996).

The wreckage was loaded into boats and helicopters from the USS *Oak Hill* (LSD 51) and later the USS *Trenton* (LPD 14) for transportation to Long Island, where a former Grumman plant was located. *Trenton* and *Oak Hill* also supported the effort with berthing for many of the divers working on *Grasp* and *Grapple*, since work and diving on both these vessels ran 24 hours a day and it was essential that divers had a place to grab some quality rest.

As with any aircraft crash, diving on TWA 800 was extremely hazardous because of shredded metal and razor sharp wreckage. Add to that hundreds of miles of control cables and wiring that could entangle a diver,

Divers leaving the surface.

compounded by the unpleasant task of recovering the numerous victims, and it becomes evident that the Navy divers had earned their place in history. Divers and support personnel worked around the clock from 18 July until the end of diving operations on 2 November, only stopping for weather. Diving operations concluded with over 95 percent of the aircraft recovered. In just three and a half months, 226 Navy divers from 23 commands had made 677 surface-supplied dives and logged 856 hours of bottom time. Along with over 100 civilian police and fire-rescue divers, Navy divers made 3,667 scuba dives and logged an additional 917 hours under often harsh conditions.

With the recovery of TWA 800, the US Navy had run point on one of the largest diving and salvage operations ever conducted and Navy divers had recovered many of the victims. The Navy had played a major role in helping the NTSB and FBI investigate a tragedy that had unprecedented national significance.

USS *MONITOR* PROJECT

In 2000, MDSU-2 became involved in another significant recovery project, but not as a result of a recent disaster at sea. This recovery was of a historical and archeological nature. With the issuance of a grant by the DOD Legacy Program, and support of Senator Warner (R-VA), the Supervisor of Diving received the much-needed funding to support the National Oceanic and Atmospheric Administration (NOAA) in the recovery of key components of the Civil War ironclad USS *Monitor*.

While being towed to North Carolina on 31 December 1862, the 987-ton armor-turret gunboat USS *Monitor* sank during a storm, taking all 16 crew with her. In 1973 the wreck was finally located off Cape Hatteras, an area often described as the "Graveyard of the Atlantic," but by then the salt water had done its work and the ironclad was badly corroded and deteriorating. Since the entire gunboat was too fragile to recover, the decision was made to salvage key parts of this historical wreck for preservation.

Using the MK 21 surface-supplied diving system, the divers on the 2000 expedition successfully cut through the propeller shaft and raised the massive screw from the *Monitor*. The 2001 expedition was much more ambitious and focused on first exposing the engine and then recovering it with a specially constructed handling frame.

In 2001 MDSU-2 was under the competent command of CDR Barbara "Bobbie" Scholley, the former Supervisor of Diving, and the *Monitor* Expedition had become a special project for Captain Chris Murray, the then current SUPDIVE. Both of these officers were not only supervising work aboard the derrick barge *Wotan* during the recovery, they were in the dive rotation taking their turn on the bottom alongside all the other 1st & 2nd Class divers. In fact, senior officers, BDOs, and Master Divers from a number of commands, including the CO of Underwater Construction Team ONE, LCDR Greg Zielinski, took their turn in the rotation to rack up valuable deep mixed-gas diving experience. If you were a Navy diver in the summer of 2001, this was the place to be.

Of all the sailors on the *Monitor* project in 2001, one diver had a truly unique and memorable experience. Fresh out of Navy dive school, this diver was to make his first real working dive with the fleet, and it was to be a deep mixed-gas dive. Where most divers' first dive would be a twenty or thirty-foot dive off a pier somewhere, EN3 Dixon was making a 240-foot mixed-gas dive on the most high-profile operation of the day. And if that wasn't enough, the dive was under the watchful eye of not only his Commanding Officer and Master Chief but also the Supervisor of Diving for the entire Navy.

EN3 Dixon.

Another unique aspect of the 2001 expedition was the Navy's decision to deploy a saturation diving system. A sat system consists of a diving bell that can be mated to pressurized living quarters, allowing the divers to remain at depth for extended periods of time. Once a diver has been at depth or under pressure for over 12 hours, his body becomes "saturated" with dissolved gases, so no matter how long the diver stays down, the decompression debt remains the same.

Much like a pressurized elevator, the sat system diving bell is used to lower the divers to the job site each day, and then return them to the living chambers for food and rest. This system enables divers to work for several hours in the water and remain at depth for up to 30 days before decompressing back to the surface.

The problem at that time was that the Navy did not own a transportable or shipboard saturation diving system. With the decommissioning of submarine rescue ships *Pigeon*, *Ortolan* and *Elk*

Global diving bell used on the Monitor *Project.*

River, in the early nineties, the Navy's MK-2 Deep Diving Systems were also retired.

To solve this problem the Navy turned to one of its civilian diving contractors. Global Diving supplied the Navy with a 1500-foot saturation system that was then refitted and certified to Navy requirements.

The saturation system was mounted on the side of the DB *Wotan*, and just down the deck from the surface-supplied dive stations. This allowed the Navy to run round-the-clock diving operations on both stations. The end result was that the Navy divers successfully recovered the engine and passed it over to John Broadwater and his NOAA team to be taken to the Mariner's Museum in Newport News, Virginia, for study, preservation, and, one day, display.

Following the model of the 2001 expedition, in August 2002 Navy divers recovered the gun turret of the *Monitor*, nearly 140 years after the historic warship had sunk during a New Year's storm. Was it worth the $6.5 million price tag? Most definitely!

Diving operations such as the *Monitor* Project are essential to the future of Navy diving. Where else can young Navy divers get the opportunity to gain deep mixed-gas diving experience, and where else will the more experienced divers get the opportunity to participate in saturation diving operations? On the 2001 expedition alone, 150 divers from 24 different commands had the opportunity to rack up some invaluable experience and mixed-gas dive time. Forty Navy divers made their first mixed-gas dive and six made their first saturation dive; eleven qualified as Fly-Away Mixed-Gas System Operators and two qualified as Unlimited Mixed-Gas Diving Supervisors. This type of operational experience is invaluable to not only Navy diving but also the US Navy's overall operational readiness. The Navy divers who worked on the *Monitor* project are now tuned up and ready for the next major deep-water disaster at sea.

MDV Steve Mulholland operates double-lock deck chamber.

Derrick Barge DB Wotan used as diving platform on the Monitor project (2001).

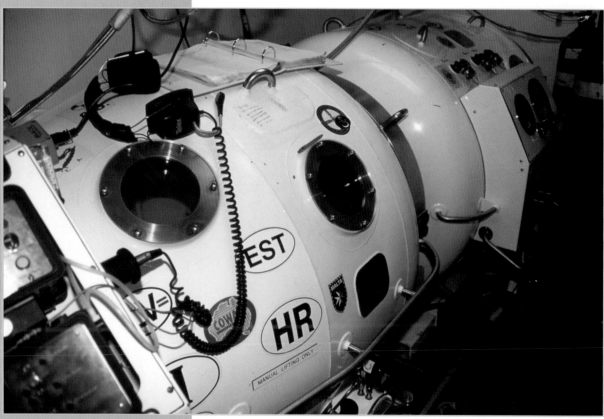

*Double-lock transportable
recompression chamber (TRCS).*

MDV Frank Perna on left.

Listening to dive brief.

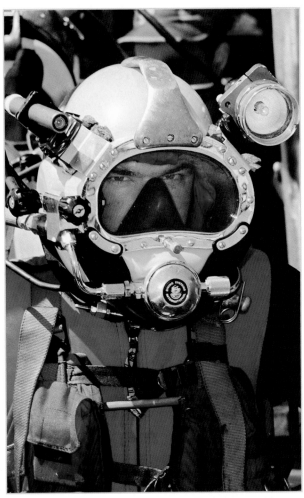

Petty Officer 2nd Class Hermanson, a diver aboard USS Grapple, *prepares for a deep dive (2001).*

Chris Murray, former SUPDIVE.

Pre-dive briefing.

MDV Frank Perna listening to pre-dive brief.

Commander Barbara "Bobbie" Scholley — former CO of MDSU-2.

Capt Chris Murray pulls his turn in the dive rotation.

Hospital corpsman (DV) Jeffrey Hajh with the MDSU-2 reserve detachment preparing to dive.

Petty Officer (DV) Neil Wolfe gives last minute instructions to the diver before a 240-foot mixed-gas dive.

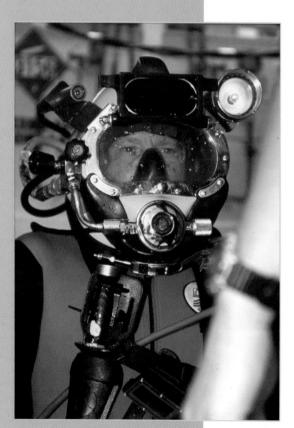

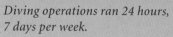
*Diving operations ran 24 hours,
7 days per week.*

*Divers descend 240' to the
Monitor (2001).*

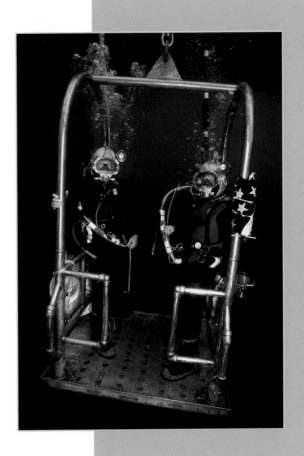

*GM1 James Burger working
a chain fall (2001).*

Saturation diver Bill Staples clearing debris from the Monitor. Note the gas reclaim modifications to the diver's helmet.

UCT diver Lowell Scrader digs around the steam condenser as he enters the bowels of the beast at 240'.

Senior Chief Bill Staples hammers away to free deck plating from the historic wreck of the USS Monitor. Staples and other saturation divers worked around the clock on this project (July 2001).

The personnel transfer capsule (PTC), saturation diving bell.

*The purpose-built handling
frame (August 2001).*

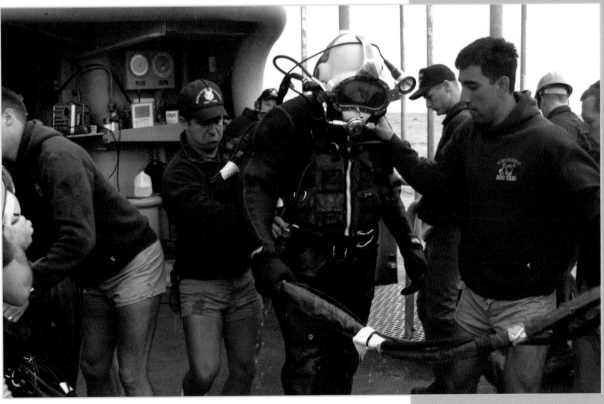

*Navy diver, Chief Photographer
Mark Reinhard, returns from a
dive aboard USS* Grapple *on the
TWA 800 recovery (1996).*

MDSU TWO command personnel.

ENDNOTES

1   Edited from MDSU2 website and unit history.
2   Edited from Grapple and Grasp command web pages.
3   "Everyday Heroes; TWA Tragedy Brings Out the Best in Navy Salvage and Diving" By Capt. Raymond Scott McCord — Supervisor of Salvage and Diving, Faceplate Summer 1997.

Underwater
Construction
Teams

"CONSTRUIMUS SUBMARE — WE BUILD UNDERWATER"

Naval underwater construction forces trace their history back to World War II, when they became involved in building coastal bases and facilities throughout the Pacific theatre. SEABEEs trained as Navy divers assigned to Naval Mobile Construction Battalions (NMCB) were used for underwater demolitions, blowing channels through reefs, and removing obstacles to shipping. Construction divers were also involved in building harbor facilities and mooring systems, much as they are today.

During the Vietnam War, Seabee divers were deployed to Southeast Asia to repair war-damaged facilities, build bridges, piers, and fuel loading docks. Construction divers were also involved in salvage operations and underwater force protection duties.

In 1969, it became evident there was need for a dedicated unit on each coast to support Fleet Underwater Construction. In 1974 the two detachments of SEABEE divers were commissioned as Underwater

CB diver Martin Stacy burning rebar with a Broco cutting torch.

Former UCT2 command staff: LCDR Brant Pickrell (R), XO Brett Blanton (Center).

Former UCT1 Commander George Zielinski.

Construction Teams with a Civil Engineer Corps (CEC) officer as the Officer in Charge. In 1985, the Underwater Construction Teams were elevated to Command status with UCT ONE homeported in Little Creek, Virginia and UCT TWO in Port Hueneme, California.

Today, Underwater Construction divers are some of the hardest working divers in the Navy. Their daily commitment to numerous harbor construction projects, repair work, and underwater inspections gives them the opportunity to rack up more dive time than just about any other diving command in the Navy.

UNDERWATER CONSTRUCTION TEAMS

Mission Statement: To provide a responsive military capability for the construction/installation, inspection, repair, and removal of ocean facilities.

Underwater Construction Teams (UCT) form components of the Naval Construction Battalions and work closely with the Naval Ocean Facilities Program (OFP) and Naval Facilities Engineering Command (NAVFAC).

A UCT has the unique capability to provide a wide range of underwater repair and construction expertise, and is truly amphibious in nature, with construction skills that include shallow and deep-water structures, mooring systems, underwater instrumentation, light salvage, and precision burning & blasting.

A UCT is capable of accomplishing both inshore and deep ocean tasks, operating as an independent unit or as augment to other organizations. The UCTs maintain three deployable Air Detachments,

Alpha, Bravo & Charlie, traveling to a dozen or more project sites during their deployment cycle.

UCT-1 is based out of the Naval Amphibious Base at Little Creek, Virginia, and has a mission of construction and demolition in a combat environment. These divers also perform construction, repair, and maintenance work on harbor installations such as piling repair and grouting, at all Naval facilities on the Eastern seaboard. Their range and capability extends from the frozen Arctic to maintaining the underwater cables and Anti-Submarine Warfare (ASW) training sensors in Hawaii.

UCT-2 out of Port Hueneme, California, has the responsibility for all ocean and waterfront facilities under the purview of Commander in Chief, Pacific (CINCPAC), which includes the Pacific Ocean, Indian Ocean, Arctic Ocean, portions of Antarctica, portions of Africa, and portions of the Middle East.

Both teams, during homeport assignment, conduct military training, advanced diver and in-rate training, commercial schools, equipment maintenance, and project planning for the next deployment cycle.

TRCS fly-away chambers.

SPECIALIZED UNDERWATER CONSTRUCTION EQUIPMENT

UCT divers use much the same equipment as other Navy divers: basic SCUBA gear, MK 21 surface-supplied systems, Fly-Away Dive Systems (FADS), and portable recompression chambers.

However, their inventory of specialized tools and construction equipment integral to their mission is quite impressive.

Light amphibious resupply craft – LARC-V.

UCT diver Joe Karr,
Gauntanamo Bay, Cuba (1997)
with hydraulic drill.

Hydraulic Tools—UCTs maintain an assortment of oil-hydraulic tools for underwater or topside use, including rock drills, impact wrenches, band saws, grinders, pile cutters, pressure intensifier, cutoff saw, and chain saw.

Hydrographic Survey—UCTs can perform hydrographic surveys using the Differential Global Positioning Systems (GPS) Hydrographic Survey System and HYPACK software, which allows survey teams to quickly prepare survey plans, perform field data collection, edit the data, and present the data in a mobile station which can be deployed in a small boat.

Water Craft—UCTs have several small boats including 25' Boston Whalers, 15' and 19' inflatable zodiacs. In addition, the Team also utilizes

Drilling to place seabed small boat moorings; Gauntanamo Bay, Cuba (1997).

larger amphibious craft called Lighter Amphibious Resupply Craft—LARC-V (pronounced "larks"), which are 35-foot wheeled vehicles capable of operating on both land and water.

Remote operated Vehicles (ROV)—UCTs are currently capable of deploying an electrically powered ROV to 500 feet vertically or horizontally.

Blasting & Demolitions—UCTs are also capable of performing precision terrestrial and underwater blasting using military or commercial explosives. Members are specifically trained to perform surgical demolition with shaped cutting charges.

Cleaning marine growth.

Changing the drill bit.

Pier and dock repair work.

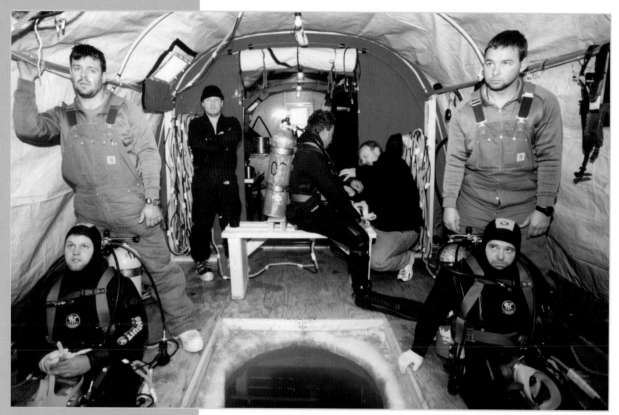

*UCTs have Arctic and Antarctic
diving responsibility.*

*Ice diving with the
MK20 AGA FFM.*

Preparing to drop beneath the ice.

Under the ice.

Explosive Ordnance Disposal

"AD BELLUM PARATI ESTE — TO BE PREPARED FOR WAR"

Explosive Ordnance Disposal, more commonly referred to simply as EOD, are the bomb technicians of the armed services. However, unlike other branches of the services, all US Navy EOD technicians are required to be divers. EOD divers receive their initial diver training at NDSTC in Panama City, but this is only the beginning of many more advanced courses in both terrestrial and underwater tools and techniques of explosive ordnance identification, handling, and disposal.

The Naval EOD mission statement is "to provide the Fleet with the capability to detect, identify, render safe, recover, evaluate, and dispose of explosive ordnance which has been fired, dropped, launched, projected, or placed in such a manner as to constitute a hazard to operations, installations, personnel, or material." The tasking extends to all explosive ordnance, from Civil War era artillery (cannon balls) to terrorist devices to nuclear weapons, particularly those which are the responsibility of the Navy or which may be discovered within the ocean, including inlets, bays, and harbors.

The focus is to enhance ship warfighting abilities and survivability by integrating EOD capabilities into Fleet Battle Groups and Amphibious

EOD diver with mixed-gas UBA.

EOD diver with MK16 Heads-Up display attached to his mask.

Ready Groups (ARG), conduct Mine Countermeasure operations, support U.S. Secret Service missions, and operate and maintain the fleet's various Marine Mammal Systems which conduct mine countermeasures, port security, and underwater object location operations.[1]

EOD HISTORY

The U.S. Navy's EOD organization evolved from the military and civilian bomb disposal units organized in Britain at the start of World War II to cope with German delay-fuse bombs and sea mines. In 1940, several U.S. Navy officers stationed in Britain were ordered to examine the German mine problem and assess British countermeasures. Upon their return to the United States in May 1941, Navy Lieutenants O. D. Waters, J. P. Roach, and S.M. Archer drew up plans for a U.S. Navy mine disposal school which was soon named the Mine Disposal School and established at the Washington, D.C., Navy Yard. Another significant figure in EOD history is Draper Kauffman, who was also active with the early UDT teams.

The first American mine disposal group was called to action soon after completing training in 1941. In the wake of the attack on Pearl Harbor, the team recovered unexploded projectiles, two Japanese torpedoes, and a 500-pound bomb. The bombs, torpedoes, and projectiles that had been rendered safe — the first Japanese ordnance to fall into American hands — were disassembled and returned to the United States for intelligence analysis and training.

At the end of the war the Chief of Naval Operations (CNO) closed the Navy's Bomb Disposal School, Mine Disposal School, and Explosives Investigation Laboratory, but the continuing need to dispose of ordnance and explosive debris resulted in the establishment of a combined, all-service Naval School Explosive Ordnance Disposal (NAVSCOLEOD) at the Naval Powder Factory, Indian Head, Maryland.

In 1947, responsibility for Explosive Ordnance Disposal training for all services was delegated to the Navy, and by 1958 the need for expanded facilities was met with new buildings for surface and nuclear training. Subsequently, a half-million gallon underwater training facility was constructed to train Naval officers and enlisted personnel in EOD diving and procedures.

In late 1971, the DOD consolidated the EOD Training and Technology Programs under the control of the Navy. To meet increased requirements for trained EOD Technicians, the CNO, in October 1985, established the Naval School, Explosive Ordnance Disposal Detachment at Eglin Air Force Base, Florida — officially opened in June 1982.

In addition to the school, the Navy needed operational EOD teams. This began in December, 1951, with the formation of Mine Disposal Unit ONE, which in 1953 was renamed Explosive Ordnance Disposal Unit ONE.

With the growth of requirements, Explosive Ordnance Disposal Group Pacific was formed in 1967 with three

Ordnance inspection by EOD divers.

Floating contact mine designed to destroy a ship.

*Navy diver Petty Officer First
Class Dean Allred returns to
surface with a piece of TWA
800 (NY, August 1996).*

subordinate commands. In 1971, this structure was modified and renamed as EOD Group ONE, with subordinate commands of EOD Mobile Unit One, EOD Shipboard Unit ONE, and EOD Training and Evaluation Unit ONE. Today EOD Group ONE consists of five EOD mobile units, one mobile diving and salvage unit, one EOD training unit, and one VSW MCM detachment.

In 1997 Naval EOD established a Very Shallow Water Mine Countermeasures (VSW MCM) detachment composed of EOD divers, SEALs, Recon Marines, an EOD marine mammal platoon and underwater autonomous vehicles (UAV). This also required the warfighting labs to develop tactics, techniques, and equipment for operating in the very demanding beach zone from the surf out to roughly 21 feet of water. This team deployed to the Gulf in 2003 as Naval Special Clearance Team ONE.

2-Alpha head gear.

EOD diver with hand-held sonar and headset searching for pieces of TWA 800 (NY, 1996).

Swimming up on a bottom anchored mine.

EOD COMMANDS

As with other commands in the US Navy, EOD is split between Atlantic Fleet and Pacific Fleet assets, with a number of satellite detachments. Explosive Ordnance Disposal Group ONE (COMEODGRU ONE) reports to the Naval Surface Force, US Pacific Fleet in San Diego administratively, and to the THIRD Fleet operationally. Based at the Naval Amphibious Base (NAB), Coronado, Group One is the operational and administrative command for four Explosive Ordnance Disposal Mobile Units (EODMU3, EODMU7, EODMU11, and EODMU17 in Oak Harbor, Washington), one Training & Evaluation Unit (EODTEU1), the administrative commander for EOD Mobile Unit FIVE in Guam, Mobile Diving & Salvage Unit ONE (EODMDSU1), and the Naval Special Clearance Team ONE (VSW MCM). Group ONE is also a component of the US Special Operations community.

With the Atlantic Fleet, the subordinate commands to Explosive Ordnance Disposal Group TWO (EODGRU2) include EODMU2, EODMU6 in Charleston, SC, EODMU8 based at NAS Sigonella, Sicily, EODMU10, EODMU12, training unit EODTEU2, and EODMDSU2.

EOD OPERATIONS

EOD divers respond to a wide variety of operations, some routine and some exigent. In the last few years, the op-tempo for EOD mobile units has increased with the added threat of terrorism. However, even with the work directly related to force protection, the EOD divers still have to respond to the needs of both the fleet and the US military as a whole.

Not all EOD operations occur under water, but the following examples are a small representation of the type of operations that require the attention of EOD divers.

In February 1999, EOD Mobile Unit 2 and SIMA divers worked together to remove 54 5-inch projectiles and powder from the forward magazine of the USS *Radford* when it had become flooded after a collision.[3]

During the Kosovo air campaign, an Air Force F-15 with an in-flight emergency jettisoned ordnance into a high altitude lake in northern Italy. Three detachments from EODMU8 responded, along with their DMO, a fly-away decompression chamber, DMTs to man it, a Master Diver, some fleet divers, and a side-scan sonar detachment.

In August 2000 Gulf Air flight 72 crashed into the sea near Bahrain and not far from the USS *George Washington*. EOD Mobile Unit 2's Battle Group Detachment, EODMU6 Mine Countermeasures, and EODMU8 Shore Detachment Bahrain all responded to the incident. They recovered the black box (FDR), debris designated by NTSB investigators, and a State Department pouch with classified material. They took photos for the NTSB, and assisted with the recovery of the remains of 143 victims.

When USS *Cole* was attacked by terrorists, October, 2000, EOD divers involved in demining operations in Yemen responded in hours, quickly reinforced by additional EOD divers working in Bahrain. When penetration into the ship was required, the EOD divers worked in support of MDSU-2 Det Alpha salvage divers.

Since 2001, EOD divers and assets have been kept busy in the Persian Gulf and surrounding waters with humanitarian demining operations and force protection duties. The mine countermeasures operations have included divers from EOD, Naval Special Warfare, the Marine Corps, and coalition military dive units from the UK and Australia.

Mine clearance training.

As can be seen by these few examples and numerous other operations, EOD divers exemplify the concept of Joint Operations. They routinely interact with other commands and diverse groups of divers to complete the mission in the most expeditious manner.

EOD TRAINING

EOD officers and enlisted train together, qualify to identical standards, and wear the same breast insignia. This shared experience creates exceptional unit cohesion within the EOD community.

Handling and disarming explosive ordnance is no simple matter, requiring many schools and courses to become a competent EOD technician. The following is a partial list of the courses taught by Naval School EOD.

EOD divers rinsing their MK16s after a dive at NDSTC.

EOD divers in training.

EOD diver approaches a bottom anchored training mine.

EXPLOSIVE ORDNANCE DISPOSAL BASIC (NAVY) is designed to train officer and enlisted personnel in the best methods and procedures for performing explosive ordnance reconnaissance, identification, access, recovery, and disposal of all conventional surface and underwater explosive ordnance and nuclear weapons, and diving related to EOD.

EOD BASIC (SURFACE) trains officer and enlisted personnel of the Army, Marine Corps, and Air Force in the best methods and procedures for performing explosive ordnance reconnaissance, identification, access, recovery, and disposal of all conventional surface explosive ordnance and nuclear weapons.

ADVANCED EOD MANAGEMENT AND TECHNOLOGY provides mid and senior level EOD technicians current training on EOD management, technological developments, updated EOD procedures, and interaction with Federal agencies.

INTERNATIONAL EOD IED/VIP ORIENTATION familiarizes selected international military personnel in the organization and training methods of Naval School, Explosive Ordnance Disposal, and the use of publications, safety precautions, special tools, and render-safe techniques employed against conventional ordnance.

RESERVE EXPLOSIVE ORDNANCE DISPOSAL APPRENTICE trains officer and enlisted Selected Reserves (SELRES) in basic demolition, ordnance location and identification, EOD detachment operational support, and EOD staff logistics support.

ADVANCED ACCESS AND DISABLEMENT is designed to train officer and enlisted personnel in the Navy, Army, Marines, and Air Force in the best methods of performing advanced explosive ordnance disposal techniques on improvised explosive devices.

EOD NAVAL RESERVE FORCES (NRF)

As with all branches of the US military, reserve forces serve as a significant component of our national readiness and force projection capabilities. Reserve EOD Mobile Units are a good example of the professionalism and readiness of the reserve EOD community.

Naval Reserve Force (NRF) EOD units are commanded by active duty EOD Officers from the 1140 (Special Operations) community. These are LCDR Command positions overseeing units comprised of active duty EOD, USNR, and Selected Reserve (SELRES) personnel.[4]

Preparing to go "in harms way."

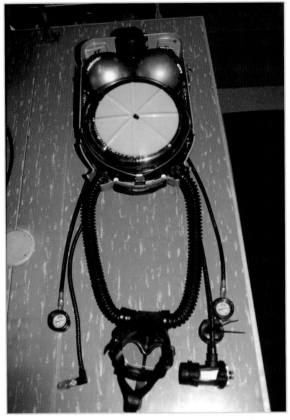

MK16 with FFM.

MK16 gas cylinders.

EOD divers doing
final bubble checks.

While the basic mission is to train Reservists, the mission is unique to Naval Reserve Force units and complimentary to their active duty counterparts. EODMU SEVEN, for example, provides a stand-alone EOD capability in support of national policy worldwide. SELRES EOD technicians can operate independently or provide a force multiplier to active duty EOD units. Through constant readiness and rigorous training, reserve EOD can create a "seamless integration" between SELRES and active duty EOD personnel available to Fleet CINCs and Operational Commanders to support their mission.

Within the EODMU OPS Department are five Ordnance Clearance Detachments (OCDs), one Area Search Detachment (ASD), one Mobile Communications Detachment (MCD), and Medical Department personnel. OCDs are normally comprised of one officer and six enlisted personnel who work together as small detachments to provide MCM diving, demolition operations, and underwater/surface ordnance clearance.

ASD operates sophisticated sonar equipment to locate underwater objects, including the acquisition/reacquisition of mine-like objects for MCM prosecution. They are a worldwide-deployable asset and are routinely called upon to provide real world support to military and civilian operations around the globe.

MCD, the mobile communications detachment, provides a highly mobile, forward deployable capability to tactical commanders and field deployed EOD units. Capabilities include HF, VHF, and SATCOM communications as well as digital imaging, facsimile, and data transmission.

The Medical Department is permanently staffed by one Independent Duty Corpsman with one SELRES corpsman assigned to provide support during drill periods. They are responsible for the scheduling and performance of routine medical requirements such as annual examinations, vaccinations, blood testing, and maintenance of CPR qualifications and medical records for all active duty and SELRES personnel. Corpsmen are trained in advance trauma response and field life support techniques, and must be able to stabilize and maintain a patient for at least six hours while awaiting MEDEVAC.

EOD DIVE LOCKER

EOD Dive Lockers maintain basic open-circuit SCUBA equipment organic to most diving commands, plus all the personal diving kit essential to EOD divers. The dive locker also maintains the primary diving rigs for EOD, the low-magnetic, acoustically silent MK-16 mixed-gas UBA. Dive locker personnel also supervise the training of EOD divers on proper maintenance and operation of these highly complex, sensor-driven diving units.

In addition to fixed systems at the command, EOD also has the Fly-Away Dive Locker (FADL) and portable recompression chambers. The FADL provides a highly mobile support unit for extended diving operations by EOD forces operating in the field or on ships away from other diving support elements.

Other important tools of the EOD divers include the underwater AN/PQS-2A hand-held sonar, flotation devices, and a variety of demolitions, disrupters, and shaped charges. The 2 Alpha allows divers to locate underwater ordnance or even relatively small objects on the seabed, even in limited to near zero visibility.

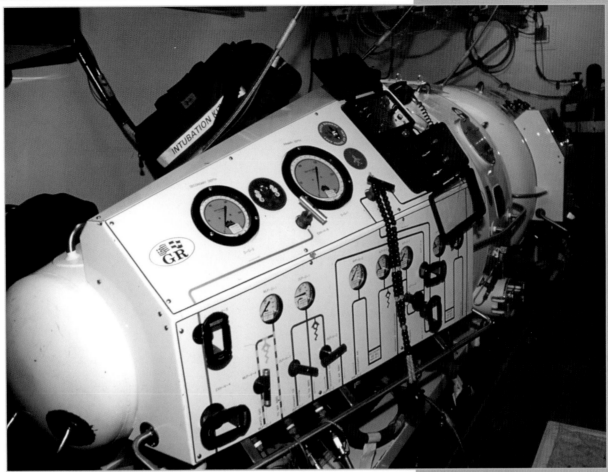

(TRCS) transportable recompression chamber system used by fly-away air detachments.

Small pin-hole shaped charges can be used to neutralize mines, and flotation devices provide the capacity to lift 2,000-pound weapons to the surface for disassembly and exploitation. If the operational objective is mine clearance rather than recovery and exploitation, MCM divers can blow in place (BIP) mines and other underwater ordnance using demolition charges. It is often necessary only to crack the case and flood the device to render it inoperable. Navy EOD MCM Dets often recover mines and devices for exploitation — to be disassembled by technicians to learn how they work.

GLOBAL READINESS

EOD prides itself on being ready for war — being strong in the right place at the right time. To achieve the command's goals, EOD has developed a response capability that is far more than just diving. Logistics, communications, combat service support, and self defense are all built into an EOD capability that is strategically mobile, flexible, agile, and sustainable. EOD assets can be anywhere in the world in 24 – 48 hours with a tailored response that is layered to escalate with the mission or the commander's needs.

LDCR Eric Anderson uses sonar to locate a bottom mine during a mine hunting exercise in the Mediterranean Sea (2000).

ENDNOTES

1   EOD Group ONE command web page
2   EOD School web page
3   Presentation by Captain Robert DeStefano, USN — Commander, EOD Group TWO since 1999
4   EODMU7 (NRF) web page

EOD divers demonstrate their air mobile static-line parachute capabilities. Many EOD Divers are also military freefall (MFF) and high altitude (HALO) jump qualified.

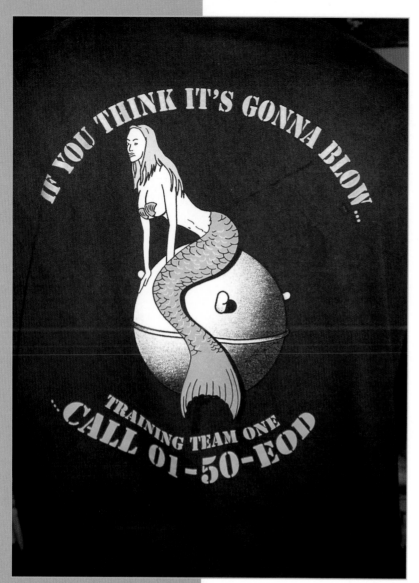

Another of the Navy diving community's colorful t-shirt designs.

Naval Special
Clearance
Team One &
Marine Mammal
Systems

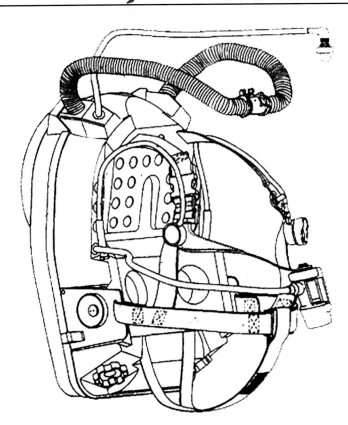

One of the challenges faced by an assault group commander planning beach landing operations is the presence of submerged enemy mines and obstacles. Even though it is doubtful the US will ever see the scope of obstacles encountered on the coast of Normandy in WWII, the modern commander must assume that the enemy has placed sub-surface mines and defenses on the approaches to beaches and harbors — at least until these have been investigated.

This is an ugly mission that requires reconnaissance teams trained in mine countermeasures and demolitions to swim in and survey the shoreline from the surf zone out to where a landing vessel may make contact with a mine anchored to the seabed. This is the zone, from roughly 10 feet out to 40 feet of depth, that is the responsibility of divers assigned to Very Shallow Water Mine Countermeasures — VSW MCM.

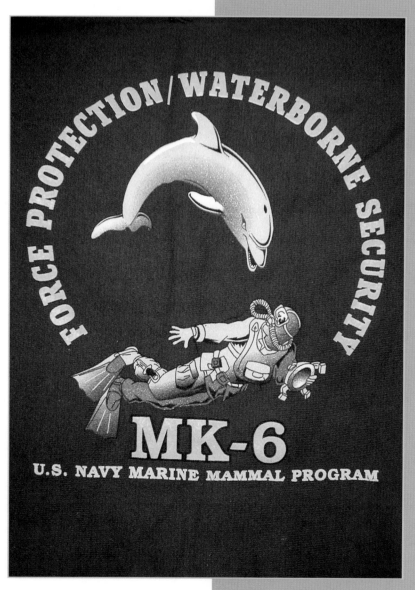

VSW MCM HISTORY & MISSION

Underwater Demolition Teams, and then SEALs, under NSW, have historically owned the mission and lead development in VSW MCM capabilities. Up to the early eighties, platoons of SEALs would deploy just outside the surf zone to try to locate simulated mines planted by evaluators. Typically one team would go in to locate the mines and map locations, to be followed by another group tasked with placing charges to blow the mines in place. The equipment used at that time was the Swimmer Area Navigation System (SANS) and the AN/PQS2A hand-held sonar.

In training exercises, swimmers were able to search the shallow waters for mines and felt confident when they found 15 out of the 20 mines placed by the training staff. But in the real world, divers may find 15 mines but not know exactly how many more remain — possibly scores or even hundreds. One tactical solution to this problem is that if the divers find any mines at all, even one, then the mission planners should look for another beach landing site where mines are not present.

*Twenty-four foot SWCC
rigid inflatable boat (RIB)
insertion craft.*

*Combat rubber raiding craft
(CRRC) piggybacking on the
SWCC RIB.*

Although the SEALs were proud of their successes in this endeavor, it was somewhat hit or miss, requiring a whole platoon to find a few targets. It became evident to Navy command that there needed to be a better way to locate and identify mines on the seabed.

Faced with the relatively primitive Iraqi mine threat in the 1991 Gulf War, the US Navy realized that it did not have the expertise to carry out this difficult mine clearance mission in the shallow water zone. Determined to find a solution to the VSW MCM problem quickly, the then Chief of Naval Operations established the VSW MCM Test Detachment in Coronado in January 1996. The "test Det" included dolphins assigned from the Navy's marine mammal program and volunteers from three elite organizations – SEALS, Marine Recon, and Navy EOD.

The reasoning behind this force structure was that the SEALs owned the mission of hydrographic survey and underwater demolitions; the Marine Expeditionary Units had the greatest interest in beach assault operations; and that EOD had the expertise in mine countermeasures and marine mammals.

This one-of-a-kind group experimented with equipment, tactics, and techniques to find mines in the VSW zone. Twenty-one months of testing resulted in the decision to establish the VSW MCM DET permanently and the command was officially established in October 1971.

SWCC boat chief.

SWCC are used to insert NSCT-1 divers.

Training off NAB Coronado.

*SWCCs will loiter in a
security posture during
clearance operations.*

CRRC are used for final beach approach to the VSW zone.

NSCT-1 divers prepare to deploy.

NSCT-1 divers ready to deploy.

Divers prepare the MK17 integrated navigational system (INSS) for mine hunting.

Pre-dive checks

*NSCT-1 divers prepare for a
VSW-MCM exercise.*

Viper with M-48 FFM.

M-48 full face mask.

The mission of the DET was to provide a small cadre of specially trained and equipped forces to conduct clandestine, low-visibility mine exploration and reconnaissance operations in the VSW zone (from 40 feet in to the surf zone). The VSW MCM Detachment would focus on development and maintenance of the following operational capabilities:

1. Confirming the presence or absence of mines in selected areas of VSW
2. Re-acquiring and identifying mine-like contacts in VSW
3. Providing the Commander, Amphibious Task Force (CATF), data from reconnaissance missions in VSW to predict the mine density
4. Enabling in-stride breaching operations by preparing or destroying large obstacles in the VSW zone.

NSCT-1 COMMAND

Naval Special Clearance Team One (NSCT-1) evolved out of VSW MCM DET and is still composed of SEALS, EOD divers & Marine Mammals, and Recon Marines. Together they form a combined operations unit tasked with clearing boat lanes of mines in the shallow water zone, as would be found on beach landing operations.

Administratively, NSCT-1 answers to Explosive Ordnance Disposal Group ONE in Coronado, California, but operationally they become a component of Naval Special Warfare Command (NSWC), also referred to as WARCOM. There has been talk of creating an East Coast team to mirror Team One, but this is not being pushed forward at time of writing.

The operational component of NSCT-1 is comprised of six platoons and a communications unit. Alpha, Bravo, and Charlie Platoons are the three dive teams, each made up of roughly 15 divers and led by a Navy Lieutenant or Marine Captain (O3).

Delta Platoon is the Special Warfare Combatant Craft (SWCC) component, made up of special warfare boat drivers and crew-served weapons operators. Their mission is to insert and extract the divers from over the horizon and handle force protection. They are currently utilizing 24-foot RIB boats with a single M-60 mount, but will be soon stepping up to specially modified 11-meter RIBs with three weapons mounts for 50 caliber machine guns and MK 19 belt-fed 40mm grenade launchers.

Echo Platoon operates the Unmanned Underwater Vehicles (UUVs), and Foxtrot Platoon, manned by Navy divers, is responsible for the Marine Mammal Systems (MMS).

Viper gas cylinders.

NSCT-1 DIVE LOCKER

In addition to basic scuba gear, wetsuits, semi-dry suits, and related diving gear, NSCT divers have a few pieces of equipment unique to their command, the first being their own diving rig. The Viper, manufactured by Carleton, is a lightweight, semi-closed-circuit rebreather with a non-magnetic and low acoustical signal, developed specifically for MCM missions. It is also a simple design, back mounted and relatively easy to dive and maintain, making it ideally suited to work in the VSW zone. The fact that the Viper is more diver-friendly and less complex than the electronically controlled MK 16 is a big plus for this rig.

NSCT runs the unit on a nitrox mix and can get three and a half hours duration out of the gas supply and carbon-dioxide absorbent, depending on depth, diver exertion, and water temperature. The minimal bubble signature emitted by the semi-closed-circuit rebreather, after being vented through a diffuser, is of little consequence, considering the openwater work environment of the clearance divers.

To enhance the comfort and safety of the Viper, the NSCT divers utilize the M48 Supermask with a specially modified mouthpiece to accommodate the surface/dive manifold and breathing hoses. They also add a custom-designed utility harness to carry the explosive charges that are needed to blow mines in place.

*The Viper CCBA with
M-48 mask.*

Another piece of equipment integral to the NSCT mine hunting mission is the MK 17 INSS— Integrated Navigational Sonar System. The INSS is hand-held forward-looking sonar that navigates by triangulation and allows the diver to scan for mines or mine-like objects. It is also capable of identifying and locating the pinger/markers dropped by the MK 8 dolphins.

UNMANNED UNDERWATER VEHICLES — UUV

As a significant advancement over the previous methods of committing large numbers of divers to swim around in the murk bumping into mines, NSCT-1 has acquired a new tool, and one that finds 100% of mine-like objects on or above the seabed — the Sculpin MK 18 Mod 0 REMUS UUV.

Based on the Remote Environmental Monitoring Unit System (REMUS) developed by Woods Hole Oceanographic Institution (WHOI) under ONR support, the Semiautonomous Hydrographic Reconnaissance Vehicle (SAHRV) system was developed by NAVSEA and the Office of Naval Research (ONR) to support Naval Special Warfare missions for the US Special Operations Command (USSOCOM).[2]

The SAHRV, more commonly called a UUV, is a torpedo-like unmanned underwater vehicle that performs hydrographic reconnaissance and side-scan sonar surveys in littoral waters, from the seaward edge of the surf zone into waters as deep as 100 meters. At 63 inches in length and 80 pounds, the vehicle is small, capable of deployment by two people, simple to program, and can be launched and recovered from a small vessel without a crane or other special handling equipment.

The UUV can operate for over 20 hours on battery before recharging and is capable of 5 knots forward speed (or over 2.5 meters per second). In addition to searching and detecting mine-like objects, the vehicle will also collect data on water current velocity, seafloor bathymetry, water temperature and salinity, and optical properties of the water.

The UUV has one significant advantage over the Marine Mammals Systems and that is the ease of deployment. A typical operational package of 4 UUVs can be deployed quickly with minimal logistical support, requiring little more than a single 20-foot container.

Even though the UUV can search, classify, and map an area, it is still not task-built for mine hunting operations. While it can scan and locate mine-like objects, it cannot find or identify buried shapes — a capability of the MK 7 MMS. Nor can a UUV neutralize mines — a dangerous task done by clearance divers. There is also some concern about what will happen to the UUV in a high-density hostile minefield when it comes in close contact with modern influence mines.

MARINE MAMMAL SYSTEMS (MMS)

Another unique capability of the US Navy's EOD community is the use of marine mammals for mine detection and fleet security. Five operational Marine Mammal Systems (MMS) have been developed to fulfill Navy requirements where hardware is inadequate or safety is an issue. Dolphins are used in MMS because of their exceptional biological sonar that is unmatched by man-made sonar in detecting objects in the water column and on the ocean bottom. Sea lions are used because of

MK6 dolphin at EODMU3 in San Diego.

EOD dolphin handlers work closely with their MK6 system.

their very sensitive underwater directional hearing and low light-level vision. Both of these marine mammal species are trainable for tasks and are capable of repetitive deep diving.[3]

The dolphins have been trained not to make contact with the mines but to place a marker near them and then alert the support team. EOD divers then move into investigate and prosecute the mine by removing it or blowing in place (BIP).

"System" is the term used for the various marine mammal programs, with each system comprised of 4 to 8 marine mammals, an Officer-in-Charge, and several enlisted personnel, including qualified trainers and handlers. All MMS are rapidly transported by aircraft, helicopter, and land vehicles with all equipment to sustain an operational deployment. When transported or maintained on ships, the mammals are housed in specially designed, large, inflatable, 20-foot diameter dolphin pools.

The safety and well-being of the mammals in transit is always a top priority for the Navy. The dolphins are accompanied by their military handlers, Navy civilian trainers, and veterinarians when they are flown on a military animal transporter in fleece-lined slings, with adequate watering. This team also stays with the dolphins during forward deployed operations to ensure that their heath and fitness is maintained.

These systems regularly participate in major Fleet exercises, and the MK 6 & 7 MMS were used to support waterside security at the 1996 Republican Convention in San Diego.

SPAWAR supports these Fleet systems with replenishment marine mammals, hardware, training, personnel, and documentation.

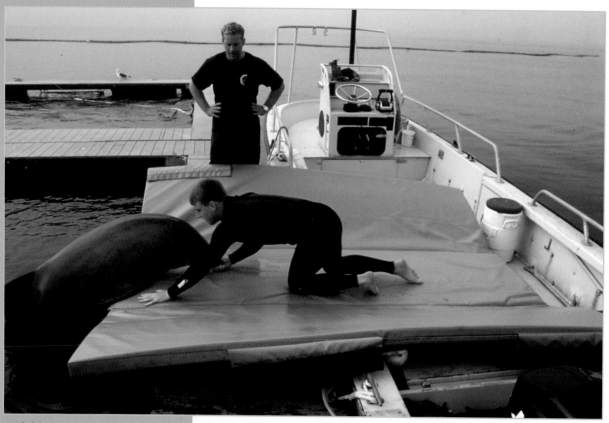

Dolphins are trained to jump into the boats for tactical deployment.

MK 4 is a dolphin mine-searching system that detects and marks locations of mines moored on the ocean bottom. It is capable of shipboard forward deployment to support post-amphibious operations.

MK 5 is a sea lion exercise mine-recovery system that locates pingered training mines. The sea lions can locate these mines to depths of 1000 feet and attach a grabber device for recovery. MK 5 systems are maintained by EODMU 3 and EODMU 6.

MK 6 is a dolphin swimmer and diver detection system that can detect and mark the location of an intruder. This system was used in Vietnam in 1970 – 71 to detect and deter sapper divers, and more recently in the Arabian Gulf.

MK 7 is a dolphin mine-searching system that detects and marks the location of mines on the ocean bottom. This system is also capable of shipboard forward deployment to support post-amphibious assaults.

MK 8 is a dolphin mine-search system trained to identify and mark mines with a pinger-locator carried in the mouth. The dolphins will drop the pinger in close proximity to the mine, allowing the divers to re-acquire the mine for prosecution.

VSW MINE CLEARANCE OPERATIONS

One of the primary tasks of the NSCT research group has been to develop the tactics and techniques for current and future mine clearance operations. Without disclosing the classified aspects of tactics and techniques that have been developed, it can be revealed that NSCT has adopted a four-phase approach to clearing beach landing lanes in the VSW zone.

Phase 1 operations extend from over the horizon (OTH), roughly 20 nautical miles out from the coast, into the 40-foot depth zone. For this phase, NSCT utilizes the MK 4 and MK 7 mammals to locate enemy mines.

In Phase 2, Echo Platoon deploys the UUVs to scan from 40 feet into 10 feet of depth, just outside the surf zone. Even though the UUV is not a dedicated mine-hunting tool, it does search the area, map the bottom, identify objects and obstructions, and collect data that will allow the mission commander to select suitable assault lanes.

In Phase 3, Foxtrot Platoon moves in with the MK 8 mammal systems to mark mines for the divers with pinger-locators. In these operations, platoon members and handlers often accompany the dolphins in special low visibility craft (LVC).

Finally, in Phase 4, clearance divers move in with hand-held sonar to re-acquire the targets and neutralize the mines with charges rigged with delay-timers. When the diving platoons move in to prosecute their mission, they are inserted clandestinely from over the horizon by the SWCC operators in high-speed RIB boats, and then complete the final approach to the VSW zone in Thunderduck 4700 wide-body CRRCs (combat rubber raiding craft).

NSCT-1 is postured to deploy within 72 hours and work from a forward operating base anywhere in the world. When deployed to the Gulf in March, 2003, UUV teams began operations within hours of getting on site, but dolphins in the MMS take longer to acclimate to their new environment.

Sea lion marine mammal system.

OPERATION IRAQI FREEDOM — 2003

When NSCT-1 deployed to the Gulf region in March, 2003, it was as part of the multinational Commander Task Unit 55.4.3 in support of Operation Iraqi Freedom. The CTU was made up of components from US Navy Special Clearance Team One, UK Fleet Diving Unit Three, Australia's Clearance Dive Team, and EOD Mobile Units Six and Eight.

In the first month, MMS dolphins cleared significant areas

The t-shirt says it all.

and investigated numerous objects in support of operations. After clearing a lane into the port for humanitarian shipping, the teams helped clear other hazards from the surrounding area, including the waterways connecting the port of Umm Qasr to the Arabian Gulf.

The team's new UUVs were also used in conjunction with the dolphins and divers in Umm Qasr and Az Zubayr and proved effective in the combined mine clearance effort. UUVs proved particularly useful by enabling the team to eliminate a large number of nonmine-like contacts.

The UUVs were deployed on 10 missions and searched 2.5 million square meters of waterways and identified 97 man-made shapes for investigation. However, until the UUVs have completed full mission profile test and evaluation, NSCT and EOD will continue to rely on the unique skills of marine mammals for MCM operations.

ENDNOTES

1   VSW MCM web page
2   Office of Naval Research - NAVSEA PMS 325J Partnership
3   EODMU3 MMS command description

Naval Special Warfare

UDT & SEAL Teams

Contrary to popular belief, Navy SEALs are not Navy divers even though they are in the Navy and dive. Where the Navy divers primarily dive and work underwater, the SEALs are special operations forces (SOF) whose job is to hunt down the enemies of the United States, kill them, and destroy their equipment. For SEAL operators, and as their acronym implies — Sea, Air & Land — diving is not a primary military occupation or job description. SEALs are also more apt to swim underwater horizontally as opposed to diving vertically.

Use of diving equipment and techniques is simply one of several methods the SEALs employ to approach a target or infiltrate into an area of operation for a mission. As such, and even though they are all trained open and closed-circuit divers, SEALs are officially designated as "Combatant Swimmers" and not Navy divers.

Unofficially, SEALs are called "frogmen" in reference to their evolution from their World War II allied and axis predecessors and the Underwater Demolition Teams (UDT). The term "frogmen" is also generically used to refer to free-swimming military divers, as opposed to the tethered hard-hat divers of the Navy's working deep-sea diver community.

Thanks in large part to exposure on the silver screen, the term "Navy SEALs" has become synonymous with military toughness, even though SEAL training and capabilities go far beyond what has been portrayed and glamorized in movies and on television. Being an SOF operator in any branch of the military is hard work, but when the mission requires an approach on, in, or under the water, a special type of mental and physical toughness is required. This ability to function in cold dark waters for prolonged periods of time is a critical component of the SEAL selection process, which is designed to ensure that an operator will not quit under combat conditions.

However, SEALs are not the only Navy personnel who dive in harm's way. In time of war the Mobile Diving & Salvage (MDSU) and Underwater Construction Team (UCT) divers play an integral role in combat operations, as do EOD divers. In fact, EOD divers work right alongside SEALs and Marine Recon combat swimmers in VSW-MCM operations to clear lanes of approach for beach landing teams.

Lightweight oxygen rebreathing swimming apparatus, which is neutrally bouyant under water (1940).

HISTORY & OPERATIONS

SEAL Teams first came into prominence in the sixties during the Vietnam War, but they can trace their lineage back to World War II (1939 – 1945). Learning from the success of Italian and British combat divers during the early days of WWII, in 1942 the Office of Strategic Services (OSS) began developing maritime units. In fact, the first US "frogman" was actually a US Navy hard-hat diver by the name of John Spence who re-enlisted for the war and was assigned to OSS to help develop assault swimmer capabilities.

The OSS was the first group to show an interest in the use of diving equipment for swimmer attack and reconnaissance operations — and well before the Navy or combat demolition teams went sub-surface.

SEAL with MP5N submachine gun.

SEAL Team 5 training in Coronado.

US Navy SEALs and Air Force pararescue jumpers (P.J.) participating in space capsule recovery.

Full tactical gear

In 1943 volunteers and demolition experts from the Naval Construction Battalions were tasked with clearing obstacles from the beaches selected for amphibious assault. This kicked off the first formal training of the Naval Combat Demolition Units (NCDU) that went on to distinguished themselves in the Pacific against the Japanese and in the Atlantic theatre against the Germans.

In the Pacific theatre, the NCDUs were consolidated into Underwater Demolition Teams (UDTs) when two newly graduated teams were sent to Hawaii in December, 1943, designated UDT 1 & 2. Their first significant mission came in support of the attack on Kwajalein in the Marshal Islands in February, 1944. The next major operation for the UDT Teams 5, 6, and 7 was the reconnaissance of Saipan beaches in the Mariana Islands in June of the same year. Two men were killed and eleven wounded, illustrating the danger of this mission, as they successfully set up the beach landing sites for the Marines.

As their web-footed brethren enjoyed the warmer waters of the Pacific, NCDU and allied commando teams were suffering in the colder waters of the North Atlantic. On June 6, 1944, at 06:33 hours, Gap Assault Team engineers and CDU11 swimmers came ashore on the beach code-named Omaha, in Normandy. Pinned down but undeterred by German machine gun fire, the men went about their task of placing explosive charges on the obstacles known as Belgian Gates. At 06:55 the charges were detonated, blasting several wide paths through the obstacles for the beach landing teams, but the price was high. Of the 175 sent ashore, 31 were killed and 60 wounded.[1]

The divers and engineers at Utah Beach had it somewhat easier, since the Germans had not expected an attack on this part of the coastline. Within 30 minutes the CDU divers had blasted eight lanes

Water jump

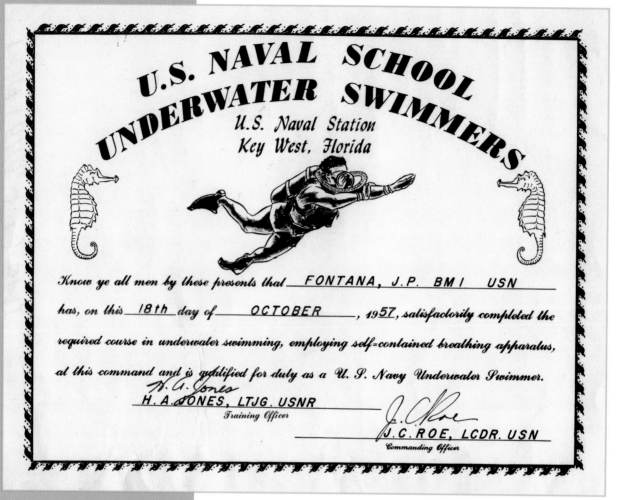

through the obstacles and another six before high tide — but unfortunately they sustained one-third casualties to enemy fire.

The survivors of Normandy and new graduates of training stateside were shipped to Maui, Hawaii, where they formed up with other units that had been serving in the Pacific. They were then officially re-designated as UDT — Underwater Demolition Teams.

UDT teams continued to see action throughout the Pacific in the Philippines, Kazan Islands, and finally Ryukyu Islands and Borneo in June, 1945. UDTs were active right up until the Japanese capitulated in August, 1945, by which time the US Navy supported some 34 UDT teams with roughly 3,500 men. But as with any post-war period, three years later there were a little more than 200 officers and men assigned to UDTs.

However, in 1947, Lieutenant Commander Doug Fane, CO of UDT 2 and famed author of the *Naked Warrior*, developed a sub-surface capability by applying SCUBA to UDT operations. Scrounging together enough gear to get started, selected men from UDT 2 and 4 were formed up into Submersible Operations Platoon (SUBOPS). With the support of COMSUBLANT and a few enthusiastic sub divers, Commander Fane and his teams began perfecting submarine lock-out and lock-in procedures.

Beginning in 1950, the UDTs were active in the Korean conflict, where they conducted coastal reconnaissance and ran sabotage and ambush operations, making use of guerilla warfare and unconventional tactics.

In 1962, the first SEAL Teams were commissioned and tasked with conducting unconventional warfare, counter-guerilla warfare, and

clandestine operations in maritime and riverine environments. At that time there were two teams formed — SEAL Team ONE on the West Coast and SEAL Team TWO on the East Coast.

During Vietnam (1967 – 1971), the SEALs continued to hone their skills while racking up an impressive record of kills and successes. It was in the Mekong Delta while inflicting heavy casualties on the Viet Cong that the SEALs became known to the enemy as the "devils with green faces." This dubious honor came with a bounty being placed on the head of any SEAL killed or captured.

Post-Vietnam, and in response to a greater demand for military special operations, the SEALs and Naval Special Warfare community have continued to expand and evolve. Part of this process included UDT teams being re-designated as SEAL or SEAL Delivery Vehicle (SDV) Teams. The newly designated SEAL Teams acquired the SEAL special operation missions while retaining the amphibious support missions required of their UDT predecessors.

NAVAL SPECIAL WARFARE COMMAND

Naval Special Warfare has undergone considerable growth in recent years. This has been driven by the need to maintain the traditional war-fighting missions plus meet the ever growing demand for special operations in the current global war on terrorism.

There are now six major commands within the Naval Special Warfare command structure. SEAL Teams One, Three, Five, and Seven fall under the command of Naval Special Warfare Group ONE, based at NAB Coronado, California.

Naval Special Warfare Center, a full command that includes BUD/S, is also co-located at NAB Coronado.

SEAL Teams Two, Four, Eight, and Ten fall under the command of Naval Special Warfare Group TWO headquartered at NAB Little Creek, Virginia. ST-10 was commissioned in March, 2002, under Group 2, the same

SEAL with MK25 rebreather and MP-5 9mm.

date that ST-7 was commissioned under Group 1 on the West Coast.

NSW Groups THREE & FOUR are the old Special Boat Squadrons now known as Special Boat Teams, manned by Special Warfare Combatant Crewmen (SWCC). Their primary function is NSW mobility and encompasses SDV teams, the newer ASDS, the Mk V Special Operations Craft (SOC), NSW RIB and tactical vehicles.

Group 3 (Coronado) commands SDV-1 (Pearl Harbor) and SBT-12, while Group 4 (Little Creek) has SDV-2, SBT-20, and SBT-22 (Stennis, MS).

The sixth Group is CNSWDG, not to be confused with ST-6 that was created after the Iranian hostage crisis in 1980, but disestablished in 1989 as the regular Teams took over the counter-terrorist mission. NSW Development Group (DEVGROUP) is a major command (O-6) that reports to Naval Special Warfare Command, as do each of our other five major commands (Groups 1, 2, 3, 4, and the Naval Special Warfare Center). NSW component commands support US Special Operations Command (SOCOM), both CONUS and OCONUS, to include operations in Afghanistan and Iraq.

SEAL Teams, SEAL Delivery Vehicle (SDV) Teams, and Special Boat Teams (SBT) comprise the elite combat units of Naval Special Warfare (NSW). These teams are organized, trained, and equipped to conduct special operations, clandestine maritime and riverine operations, foreign internal defense, and unconventional warfare.

RECENT OPERATIONS

SEAL Teams were active in Beirut in the early eighties and played a role in Operation Urgent Fury, Grenada, in October, 1983. A SEAL team en-route to Lebanon was re-routed to Grenada to support the invasion operations where SEALs were given three missions. The first was the reconnaissance of Pearl's Airport and beach. Sadly, four

SEALs are supported by special boat teams (SBT).

SEALs were lost on a night parachute drop into rough seas. The second mission was the destruction of the Cuban-built Radio Free Grenada transmitter. The third was the rescue of British Governor-General Sir Paul Scoon, where members of the highly classified SEAL Team 6 fast roped in to secure his safety.[2]

In December 1989, in support of Operation Just Cause to arrest Panamanian dictator General Manuel Noriega, SEAL Teams TWO and FOUR were tasked with two primary missions. The first was a true frogman operation — to disable Noriega's 65-foot yacht, the *Presidente Porras* which was also equipped as a gunboat and posed a threat to US troop aircraft passing overhead. Supervised by SEAL Team TWO Commander Norm Carley, four operators were selected for the task — EM3 Timothy Eppley, PH2 Christopher Dye, LT Edward Coughlin, and Chief Randy Beausoleil[3]. Under cover of darkness the two 2-man teams successfully entered the harbor on closed-circuit rebreathers and placed explosive charges under the ship. After setting the timers for 45 minutes, the SEALs exfiltrated to the agreed rendezvous with Commander Carley, waiting with the CRRCs, the SEALs, having used almost twice the amount of explosives necessary sunk the ship and the mission was deemed a success.

The second mission was also successful but cost a high price when SEALs from Team FOUR were sent to seize Paitilla Airfield and disable Noriega's private jet, a kind of mission usually given to Rangers. Because of restrictive rules of engagement and concerns for collateral damage, the SEALs were not able to approach the task in the manner in which they were trained and equipped. But not wanting to lose the mission, and contrary to SEAL standard operating procedure of stealthy small unit operations, the SEALs ended up going in with sixty men to do a task for which the army would use two to three hundred.

To further throw the SEALs off their game, and after they had already loaded into their boats, there was a change in orders. Less than an hour before H hour, the SEAL commander received word that Noriega's jet was not to be shot-up from a safe distance by rifle fire, but that the SEALs were to enter the hangar and disable it. This meant moving out into the open where the SEALs were not comfortable — but true to form they adapted and continued the mission.

With H hour moved up to 12:45 a.m., to coincide with a Delta rescue operation at the Modelo Prison, the SEALs came in across the beach in sixteen boats — three SEAL platoons, a headquarters platoon, a mortar squad, and two Air Force combat controllers with an AC-130 gunship circling overhead. Golf platoon took the lead, flanked by Bravo and Delta platoons with the headquarters platoon pulling rear security.

Normally SEALs would send two or three men forward to scout the location, but there was some urgency because of radio intercepts indicating that Noriega may be heading to Paitilla. As Golf platoon crossed the airfield and approached the hanger they were met by heavy ground fire. Caught in the open at relatively close range, they were easy targets for the Panamanian gunmen hidden in the darkness behind solid cover. The SEALs took several casualties in the first engagement.

The SEALs responded with everything they had and called in AC-130 Spectre gunship support, but four SEALs were killed and eight others wounded.

SEALs tranfer by fast rope to a nuclear submarine.

The SEALs were ultimately successful, but this was one mission they would be debriefing in detail for the important lessons learned.

During Operation Desert Shield (late 1990) and Operation Desert Storm (early 1991) the SEALs under the overall command of Captain Ray Smith had a number of missions. The first was to prepare a hostage evacuation plan for the US Embassy in Kuwait, and the recapture of the Embassy compound if it was overrun. SEALs would also be tasked with laser designation of key Iraqi targets for US and Coalition smart bombs, along with combat search and rescue (C-SAR) missions for downed pilots.

One of the first direct action missions the SEALs executed was the snatch of Iraqi prisoners from a small island off Kuwait City, where they killed three and captured twenty-nine. But the most successful "frogman" mission was the coastal deception run by LT Tom Deitz[4] and his small group of SEALs. They probed the southern beaches, setting explosive charges with timers, and convinced the Iraqis that the United States Marines would assault from the sea. This drew Iraqi forces, resources, and attention away from the sweeping armored attack that actually came out of the western desert, destroying and cutting off the retreating Iraqis.

Along with assets from Marine Force Recon, and a handful of Green Berets, the SEALs also participated in the famous battle for Ras Al Khafji. As the Iraqi 5th Mechanized Infantry Division pushed south from Kuwait into the Kingdom of Saudi Arabia, it was a small handful Marines and SEALs that stayed in place to report on enemy movements and vector in

Marine Cobra attack helicopters and Air Force A-10A Warthogs. Between their courage and US airpower, the Iraqi tanks and mechanized infantry were shredded, breaking the back of the Iraq advance.

From 1991 to 2001, the SEALs were active in Operation Provide Comfort in northern Iraq, in counter-drug operations in Central and South America, and in support of US and NATO operations in Bosnia and Kosovo. From 2001 to 2005, the SEALs have been active in Operation Enduring Freedom and Operation Iraqi Freedom—both ongoing operations at the time of writing (see Chapter 21).

SEALS & NAVY DIVING

Diving is not only a historical part of UDT/SEAL operations, it is still an integral component of their current mission requirements. Surface and sub-surface maritime operations are still the "bread & butter" of the Naval Special Warfare community. However, with the ever changing nature of special operations, and the range of skills and diversity in training that this requires, diving is now only one of many specialized skill-sets that the SEALs must maintain.

In addition to combat swimming and amphibious operations, SEALs strive to gain and maintain proficiency in all aspects of land-based military special operations, and in more recent years counter-terrorism. To become a well-rounded SEAL operator requires years of intense training that encompasses advanced infantry skills, demolitions, communications, military free-fall parachuting, desert operations, jungle warfare, urban warfare, survival, escape & evasion, cold weather warfare, mountain warfare, helicopter

SEALs operating from a sub.

deployment, special weapons training, small unit tactics, sniper, counter insurgency, maritime interdiction, VBSS, counter-hijacking, and hostage rescue.

In all of these specialized areas of training and operations, and since the actual SEAL operators are relatively few in number, Naval Special Warfare employs highly trained support personnel to assist with logistics, transportation, and communications. One of these support groups is the Navy divers attached to SEAL and SDV Teams.

To support the SEAL Teams in their operations, and to allow the SEAL operators to concentrate on vital mission planning and objectives, teams of highly motivated Navy divers and technicians handle many of the diving related tasks, such as dive equipment maintenance, preparation, submarine lockouts, and the launch and recovery of SEAL Delivery Vehicles (SDVs) from Dry Deck Shelters (DDS) (see Chapter 15 for SDV operations).

"We are augmented in a significant way by fleet divers at all classes, at all experience levels, and without the fleet divers Naval Special Warfare could not accomplish its mission." — RADM Eric T. Olson, Naval Special Warfare[5]

ENDNOTES

1 SEALS, The US Navy Commandos by Eric Micheletti
2 The reader can learn more about this operation in the book "ONE PERFECT OP" by Command Master Chief Dennis Chalker USN (Ret)
3 Brave Men –Dark Waters – Orr Kelly 1992
4 Later to become CDR Deitz, CO of ST-5
5 Future of NSW Forces Under the Sea, keynote speaker, RADM Eric Olson

SEALs prepare Zodiac Combat Rubber Raiding Craft (CRRC) on the deck of a submarine.

Navy Divers.

Returning to the DDS.

"Where was that hatch?"

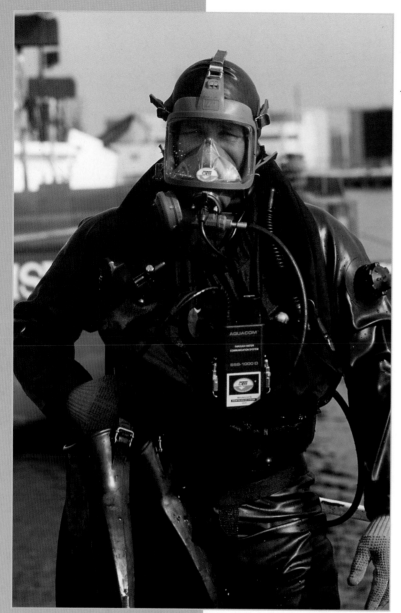

SEALs and SDV divers utilize Ocean Technology Systems (OTS) SSB-1000 underwater communication systems in conjunction with the AGA and M-48 full face masks.

Basic Underwater Demolition/SEAL Training

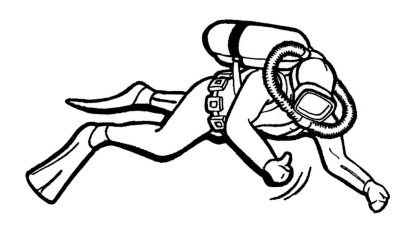

"WHERE THE ONLY EASY DAY WAS YESTERDAY"

Any sailor who is a US citizen, 28 years old or younger, in good physical condition, has eyesight correctable to 20/20 with no color blindness, and can pass a dive medical examination can try out for Basic Underwater Demolition/SEAL program — known simply as BUD/S. That's right, not directly to SEALs, to BUD/S.

A sailor who hopes to become a SEAL must first meet the basic physical requirements just to be considered for BUD/S, then survive the 17 weeks of pre-conditioning and first phase training, including Hell Week, just to make it to the dive training. After another 7 weeks of dive training and 10 weeks of land warfare training, the aspiring SEAL candidate may just be in sight of graduating BUD/S and beginning his career track in Naval Special Warfare — but still not a SEAL. It will take months of advanced training with his assigned platoon, airborne parachute training, and the approval of his peers to actually become a full-fledged SEAL and wear the coveted Trident.

BUD/S COURSE DESCRIPTION

As the official warning order states, "the key to success at BUD/S is proper preparation prior to arrival." BUD/S candidates must be physically

It all begins with basic fitness and swimming.

BUD/S candidates.

Scuba training.

fit and self-motivated. From Day One the Navy begins to test the candidates' mettle to see if they are ready to "be someone special"!

BUD/S indoctrination is two weeks in length and includes a mandatory course designed to give the student an understanding of the techniques and performance required. The first obstacle a student faces is the BUD/S Physical Screen Test (PST) which he must pass in order to class up and begin training. The test consists of a series of exercises with short rest periods in between:

- 500-yard swim using breast and/or sidestroke in 12.5 minutes
- Minimum of 42 push-ups in 2 minutes
- Minimum of 50 sit-ups in 2 minutes
- Minimum of 6 pull-ups — No time limit
- Run 1.5 miles wearing boots and long pants in 11.5 minutes

FIRST PHASE — BASIC CONDITIONING

After additional pre-training, First Phase is eight weeks in length, during which continued running, swimming, and calisthenics grow increasingly difficult. Students participate in weekly 4-mile runs in boots and timed obstacle courses. They swim ocean distances up to 2 miles in fins, and learn small boat seamanship.

The first 4 weeks of First Phase prepare the trainees for the fifth week, known as "Hell Week." Students participate in five and a half days of continuous training, with a maximum of 4 hours sleep for the entire week. This week is designed as the ultimate test of physical and mental

Swimming with side stride.

motivation while in First Phase. During Hell Week, trainees will learn the mainstay of the SEAL Teams — TEAM WORK!

The remaining 3 weeks are devoted to learning methods of conducting hydrographic surveys and preparing hydrographic charts. This continued time in the cold waters off San Diego tests the trainees' ability to function in cold, dark waters for prolonged periods of time. This is a critical component of the SEAL selection process and is designed to ensure that an operator will not quit under combat conditions.

SECOND PHASE — DIVING

By completing First Phase, the students have proven to the BUD/S instructor staff that they are motivated to participate in more in-depth training. The Diving Phase is 7 weeks in length, and physical training continues during this period, with the times being reduced for the 4-mile run, 2-mile swim, and dreaded obstacle course.

In addition to all the essential academics required in any basic diving program, Second Phase concentrates on combat SCUBA (Self-Contained Underwater Breathing Apparatus). Students are taught two types of SCUBA: open circuit (compressed air) and closed circuit (100% oxygen), the latter being the MK 25 rebreather used for most combat diving operations.

Divers participate in a progressive dive schedule emphasizing the basic combat swimmer tactics and techniques necessary to qualify as a combat diver. These skills will enable them to operate tactically, to complete their combat objective, and are the fundamental skills that separate SEALs from all other special operations forces.

Boat crews.

Boat drills.

Pool training.

Problem solving.

Beach P.T.

THIRD PHASE — LAND WARFARE

The land warfare phase is 10 weeks long, covering basic infantry type skills, demolitions, reconnaissance, weapons, and tactics. The physical training also grows more strenuous as the run distances increase and minimum passing times are lowered for the runs, swims, and obstacle course.

Third Phase concentrates on teaching land navigation, small-unit tactics, rappelling, conventional military and underwater explosives, and weapons training. The final 4 weeks of Third Phase are spent on San Clemente Island, where students apply the techniques acquired throughout training in a practical environment.

POST-BUD/S SCHOOLS

BUD/S graduates receive 3 weeks of basic parachute training at Army Airborne School, Fort Benning, Georgia, prior to reporting to their first Naval Special Warfare Command. Navy Corpsmen who complete BUD/S and Basic Airborne Training also attend 2 weeks of Special Operations Technician training at the Naval Special Warfare Center, Coronado. They also participate in an intense course of instruction in diving medicine and medical skills called 18-D (Special Operations Medical Sergeant Course). This is a 30-week course where students receive training in treating all manner of combat injuries including burns, breaks, gunshot wounds, and trauma.

After assignment to a Team and successful completion of a six-month probationary period, qualified personnel are awarded a Naval Special Warfare Classification Code and Naval Special Warfare Insignia.

Survival swimming.

Dive checks.

Wetsuits worn under BDUs.

Beach recon exercise.

*SEALs prepare to deploy
from Zodiac, F-470.*

New combat swimmers serve the remainder of their first enlistment (2.5 to 3 years) in either an SDV or a SEAL Team.

As a SEAL's career progresses, a broad range of advanced "high speed" training opportunities are available to him, including: Sniper School, Military Freefall, HALO/HAHO, VBSS, Dive Supervisor, Counter Terrorism, Advanced Diving, Advanced Tactical Shooting, language training, SEAL tactical communications, Mountain Warfare, Assault Climbing, and the list goes on.

In addition to normal pay and allowances, qualified Naval Special Warfare personnel receive additional bonuses for hazardous duty, such as: $175 per month dive pay, $300 per month SDV pay, $150 per month jump pay, $225 per month HALO (jump pay), $150 per month demolition pay, $110 per month special duty assignment pay, and $50 to $100 per month language proficiency pay for those speaking a second language. Add all those up and SEALs are making considerably more than the average sailor — but then, they are far from average!

DIVING EQUIPMENT

Basic open-circuit SCUBA equipment is used by SEALs and attached Navy divers for numerous applications such as locking in and out of submarines and the launch and recovery of SDVs. However, the bubbles emitted by open-circuit equipment all but negate its use for covert combat missions and stealthy approach swims.

The basic closed-circuit rebreather used by the SEALs, as with most special operations units, is the MK 25, more commonly known as the Drager LAR-V. The MK 25 is a simple, lightweight rebreather that is worn on the chest and utilizes 100% oxygen. But since pure oxygen becomes toxic at depth, the MK 25 is limited to shallow water swims, in the fifteen to twenty-foot range.

For deeper applications the SEALs and SDV operators use the MK 16—a fully closed-circuit mixed-gas rig capable of dives to 300 feet with the correct gas mixture. The MK 16 can also be used in conjunction with the MK 24 or newer M48 full-face mask, giving better thermal protection and the capability of underwater communications.

Artwork By "Pirate Pete"
Carolan, US Navy SEAL (USNR).

SDV Teams & Navy Divers

SEAL Delivery Vehicles

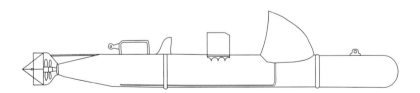

15

"TO BE WHERE WE'RE NOT EXPECTED TO BE, WITH CAPABILITIES WE'RE NOT EXPECTED TO HAVE"

SEAL Delivery Vehicles (SDV), essentially wet mini-submarines, are such an interesting component of Naval Special Warfare that it would not be difficult to write an entire book about these unique craft and the hardy individuals who operate them.

Once a highly classified capability, the SDV commands have come out of the shadows and allowed the SDVs to be photographed, restricting only images of the internal controls and advanced navigational electronics. The only other aspect of SDVs that is not discussed is the range and operational capabilities of the boats.

HISTORY & DEVELOPMENT OF THE SDV

As with modern combat diving, swimmer delivery vehicles have evolved from the underwater "pigs," "chariots," "X-craft," and midget submarines developed by the Italians and British during World War II. Designed to enhance the combat diver or saboteur's capability, early mini-subs were able to travel further than a diver could be expected to swim and carry a considerably larger demolition charge.

Though crude by modern standards, often little more than a torpedo with manual controls, when combined with commando divers on closed-circuit rebreathers, these primitive underwater vehicles were the essence of stealth and destruction. They could penetrate harbor defenses and deliver a 300-pound warhead under enemy warships.

Although special operations forces have many methods of insertion, ranging from night free-fall parachuting to high performance all-terrain vehicles, there is no more

SDV being loaded aboard a nuclear submarine.

SDV on the surface.

stealthy approach than underwater. Conventional submarines have also long been used to transport commandos, resistance personnel, reconnaissance teams, and intelligence officers to enemy shores, but these large boats are limited by size and depth to how close they can approach the beach. Sub commanders are also hesitant to take their submarines into shallow waters where they are more easily detected and maneuvering is limited.

To keep the sub in deep water where it can lurk undetected or dive in an emergency meant that naval commandos were faced with a long cold swim or an exposed transit to the shore in rubber boats or canoes. To bridge this gap the Navy developed the SDV.

In 1952, a confidential naval report stated, "when it is necessary to operate near an enemy-held shore in as complete secrecy as possible, the approach to the objective must be made underwater, and in the final leg must be made by swimming or in a small submersible. Moreover, since many coasts throughout the world have shallow gradients, scuba-equipped combat swimmers would run out of gas and/or be overly fatigued without benefit of a small powered submersible."[1]

Over the next two decades over thirty different versions of SDVs and diver propulsion vehicles were designed or tested, including the Trask, the Sea Horse and the Aquabat, but it wasn't until 1968 that the four-man MK VII was approved and put into service with the SEALs.

SDV launch.

Then in the mid-seventies, under the technical direction of Coastal Systems Station (CSS), Ken Specht and his crew at China Lake developed two new SDVs — the MK VIII and the MK IX boats. The larger SDV Mark 8 became the primary underwater SEAL delivery platform for the next twenty years, while the two-man Mark 9 reconnaissance vehicle remained in service until 1991 but was never fully optimized.

For underwater navigation, the SDVs utilized Doppler inertial navigation systems and obstacle avoidance sonar. Both worked well, allowing the SDVs to be piloted into narrow shipping channels, but the Mark 9 was to be fitted with side-looking sonar which would have greatly enhanced its capabilities for reconnaissance, hydrographic survey, and even mine hunting. Unfortunately the project died because of lack of administrative drive to make this a reality.

CSS continues to maintain a support infrastructure for SDV T&E, modifications and updates, port facilities, equipment to handle the SDV deepwater test range, and facilities to handle SDV operators and support personnel.

In 1995, the MK VIII boats underwent a service-life extension program (SLEP) that significantly upgraded their operational capabilities. These upgraded MK VIIIs are the vehicles that continue to service the SDV Teams to date, but the biggest challenge facing the SEALs is not technological but environmental. Since SDVs are "wet" subs, the pilots and guys in the back are exposed to extremes in temperature, resulting in hypothermia and potentially serious physical debilitation.

SDV Team 1 in Pearl Harbor, Hawaii.

SEAL SDV TEAMS

Drawing an assignment to an SDV Team is one of the toughest missions for Navy SEALs. Being an SDV pilot, or even just being one of the SEALs sitting in the back, is a love-hate relationship. The SEALs appreciate the fact that the SDV extends their underwater range and saves them long, exhausting approach swims, but they dread the long transits just sitting in the SDV in frigid waters. At least when swimming the exertion generates heat to keep them warm, but sitting motionless for hours is both mind numbing and physically demanding.

When running Northern European or North Korean profiles, the SEALs are subjected to water temperatures in the 28 – 35 degree (F) range for hours on end (32°F is freezing). Even with dry suits and good insulation, SDV training off Keyport, Washington, has taken the SEALS to the very limits of human endurance and, in some cases, beyond. Conversely, SEALs operating in the Persian Gulf have to deal with water temperatures above 90 degrees, resulting in extreme fatigue, dehydration, and heat stroke. These are all problems that have been addressed over the last few years in research at NEDU.

In DDS-launched SDV operations, it is not unusual to be in the water for over an hour during the SDV launch procedure, 45 minutes after flood up, followed by a possible two to three-hour transit to the beach and another two to three hours back to the sub. SDV SEALs tell stories of having spent eight to twelve hours in the water on these cold, dark mission profiles that bring flash-backs of BUD/S and severely test their ability to function when hypothermic.

Apart from being just cold, there are additional dangers associated with SDV operations. The mother sub could get pulled to the surface or have to make an emergency dive. The SDV could lose power and buoyancy and sink out of control, all of which require that the SEALs and divers bail out quickly. And to top it all off, there are a myriad of opportunities for industrial type injuries such as crushed fingers, especially during launch and recovery operations in the dark and numbing cold.

The US Navy primarily has two SDV teams and a training detachment. SEALs learn MK16 and SDV operations at the SDV R&D Dive Locker at Coastal Systems Station, Panama City. This is conveniently adjacent to NEDU and NDSTC. SEALs then receive additional training when they arrive at their assigned SDV team.

In the DDS.

Although the launch and recovery of SDVs is usually handled by Navy divers, the SEALs also learn the Dry Deck Shelter (DDS) and launch procedure in case they are not on the mission and need to assist the launch team. This DDS training is done at SDVT1 or SDVT2.

SDVT1 is located at Pearl Harbor in Hawaii where the warm clear waters provide a good training environment. However, SDVT1's regional responsibility extends all the way to North Korea, where the coastal waters are extremely cold.

SDVT2 is located at the Naval Amphibious Base Little Creek, Virginia. SDVT2, as with other East Coast teams, seems to have more experienced operators. The CO would actually prefer that all new arrivals were experienced and seasoned SEAL operators, but he can often receive SEALs straight from BUD/S.

SDV Team 2 at NAB Little Creek, VA.

DDS before flood up.

SDVT2's regional responsibility extends across the Atlantic to Europe, where they have pre-deployed assets and a 30-man Task Unit package with 10 Navy divers in Rota, Spain.

NAVY DIVERS & SDV TEAMS

As with all SEAL commands, the SDV commands are heavily augmented by support personnel and technicians who are not SEALs. One such group is the Navy Divers who, as the Commanding Officer of SDVT2 stated, "are a vital component of the SDV program."[2] At SDVT2, 20% of the command is composed of fleet divers, totaling 28 Navy divers. SDVT1 in Hawaii usually carries 40 Navy divers and a Master Diver to support SDV operations.

Having Navy divers handle all the mission support tasks such as setting up diving equipment, preparing the Dry Deck Shelter (DDS), and then launching and recovering the SDVs leaves the SEALs free to focus on the planning, approach, and combat aspects of their mission. The Navy divers, to be honest, are also better at working underwater. The SEALs may

(Continued pg 233)

Flooded DDS.

SEALs prepare their equipment in the DDS.

Ready to lock-out.

be in better physical condition and able to swim long distances, but to them diving is just a way to get to the target. Navy divers, on the other hand, who support SPECWAR operations, just live and breathe diving. Even the SEALs will be first to admit that the Navy divers know the systems better than anyone. This makes the SEALs feel safer and more confident when strapping on a rebreather and during underwater launch and recovery operations.

Navy divers receive their training in DDS and SDV launch and recovery operations at the SDV commands. This training, under the supervisions of a Senior Chief, DDS Operations & Training Officer, is quite intense and takes about 6 months. The divers receive one week of DDS classroom training and must then stand three supervised watches at each of the numerous DDS launch stations while under instruction. After this, the diver should be able to man any station during the launch and recovery of an SDV. At SDVT2 the DDS Department Head is a Chief Warrant Officer who can also serve as the Diving Officer.

*Top picture shows the half
flooded dive control bubble.*

As with all SEAL operations, SDV teams are very flexible in how they deploy and the platforms they deploy from. When SDVT2 deploys as a Task Unit (TU), the package is made up of 30 men, including ten Navy divers. SDVT1 will deploy a Task Element (TE Pacific) of one SEAL platoon and one DDS platoon.

Just to launch an SDV from a DDS underwater requires 13 manned stations, seven of which are wet, requiring divers. At the submarine's Con will be the Shelter Officer, a Master Diver (MDV), the Dive Supervisor, an E7 or above, the Log Keeper, and the Diving Medical Officer (DMO). There will also be an Air Station Operator in engineering, a position that can be handled by the sub crew.

In the DDS there is the Hanger Operator, who serves as the eyes and ears of the Dive Supervisor; the Hanger Supervisor, the Trunk Operator (1C or 2C Diver), the Chamber Operator, the Diving Medical Technician, the Deck Captain (2C Diver), and the Deck Crewman (2C Diver).

SDV Technicians will prep the SDV while the shelter is dry, then the SEALs will move all their gear up in preparation for the mission launch. After flood-up, the actual SDV launch is made from periscope depth — about 30 feet at the DDS. During the flood-up and launch the divers will usually wear 6.5mm wet suits with flight suits over the top, then breathe from hooka lines or SCUBA tanks. A routine launch takes about 1.5 hours, 45 minutes from flood up, and the divers have a max dive time of 200 minutes.

For recovery operations, the divers get the SEALs in first and out of the way, then move the SEALs' gear as far forward as possible to the front of the hangar. This leaves room to get the SDV into the DDS. Recovering the CRRCs is more difficult, requiring that the valves in the back of the boats be opened so that the rubber boats can deflate as the divers winch them down into the hangar bay. Once everything is in, the door is secured and the hangar can be de-watered.

SUBMARINES & DRY DECK SHELTERS

Any submarine can be employed to carry SEALs, however, the US Navy has several submarines that have been specially modified to carry combat swimmers and their equipment more effectively. This includes the installation of external chambers called Dry Deck Shelters (DDS) to house SDVs and additional equipment.

The DDS is essentially a large pod fitted just aft of the submarine's sail structure and mated to a hatch that provides dry access to and from the DDS while the submarine is underway. These DDSs are air transportable and can be fitted in about 12 hours.

The DDS is a cylinder 9 feet in diameter, 38 feet long, and is comprised of three interconnected steel chambers housed within a fiberglass shell. Each compartment is capable of independent pressurization to a depth of 130 feet.[3] The forward-most compartment, a sphere, is the recompression chamber used for treatment of injured divers. The middle compartment is the transfer trunk through which operators enter and exit the submarine or cross between the other compartments. The rear compartment is the hangar, which houses the SDV, or up to 20 SOF personnel with combat rubber raiding craft (CRRC). On the back end of the hangar is a massive steel door secured by heavy dogging bolts, and in the front, behind a plexi-glass shield, are the hangar operator's stations.

Navy divers assigned to SDV Team 2.

Navy divers learning DDS operations.

SDV maintenance.

Portable recompression chamber.

Two DDS shelters can be installed aboard *Benjamin Franklin* Class submarines, providing more room and flexibility as an SOF platform. This added capability also provides a level of redundancy for mission planning and contingencies. With dual hangars, one DDS can be loaded with an SDV and the other with CRRCs. This offers the flexibility to conduct SDV operations, mass swimmer lockouts, or both. Dual hangars would also allow for missions requiring two SDVs.

Redundancy is always a consideration in special operations, especially when Murphy raises his ugly head. With dual DDSs, each one interfaces with the submarine independently, so a malfunction or breakage on one system would not necessarily result in aborting the mission. The mission could continue as efforts were made to repair the inoperable DDS, even if it meant scavenging parts from one to ensure the other was fully functional.

The SEALs have a few options when it comes to deploying from a DDS. They can do a mass-swimmer lockout (MSLO), they can deploy rubber boats to the surface, or they can launch SDVs. In each case, when the submarine arrives on station at an objective, the SEALs climb from the submarine up into the

USS Grayback.

DDS, seal the hatches to the submarine, flood the DDS, open the large hangar doors and exit into the ocean. But it is not quite all that easy.

Launch operations are usually run from 30 feet, with the sub moving forward at 1–1.5 knots, and take about an hour and a half. However, there is a very long and detailed checklist to go through before the DDS can be flooded or opened to the ocean. The launch requires considerable communication between the Shelter Officer in the Con, the Hangar Supervisor and Hangar Operator in the DDS, the Trunk Operator, the Sub commander, and submarine engineering. These procedures have been put in place to protect both the integrity of the submarine and the divers. No submarine commander wants to risk his multi-billion dollar boat by having the wrong hatches or valves opened at the wrong time.

With an expected service life of at least 40 years, DDSs will continue to support SEAL and SDV missions for many years to come. However, the Navy has developed two new tools to enhance SPECWAR operational capabilities. The New Attack Submarine is designed to support the full spectrum of Special Operations missions and comes fitted with a nine-man lock-out/lock-in chamber. The other development is the Advanced Swimmer Delivery System (ASDS) — a ten-man dry mini-sub that can also lock onto a mother submarine much like the DSRV.

Navy divers are critical to DDS and SDV operations.

DDS loaded aboard nuclear submarine in Hawaii.

Dry deck shelter.

Sub with DDS put to sea.

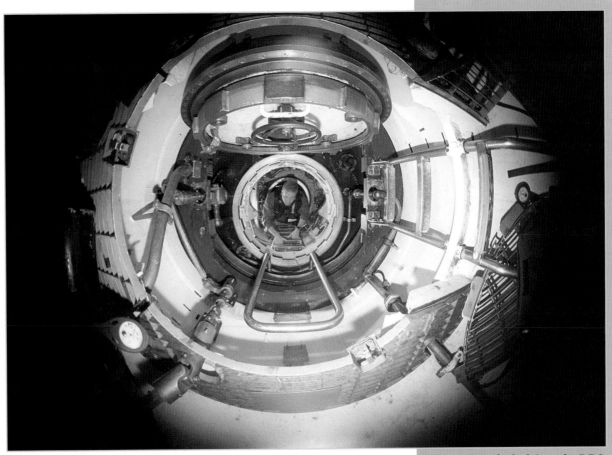

Transfer lock into the DDS.

Transfer lock.

Decompression chamber.

Main door to the DDS.

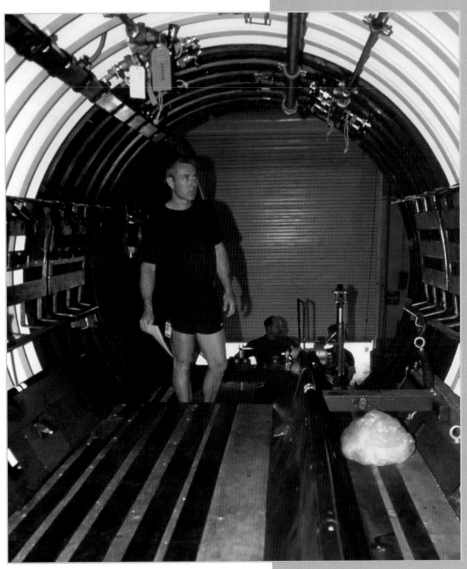

SDV storage area.

Preparing for recovery.

Navy diver assists SDV recovery.

SDV on the handling cradle.

SDV launch.

"Okay."

ADVANCED SEAL DELIVERY SYSTEM — ASDS

The SEALs have long understood the value of having a "dry" submarine, small enough for special operations that could carry a team of SEALs in relative comfort and loiter in shallow hostile coastal waters. However, the project was somewhat delayed over the fact that although the SEALs could own their own "wet" SDVs, a mini-sub that was dry on the inside would fall under the control of the Submarine Command (COMSUB). In addition, without the full support and funding of the Navy and US Special Operations Command (USSOCOM), SPECWAR would not have had the resources to develop and run with the program.

Long story short, USSOCOM came up with the funding, a contract was awarded in FY1994, and in 2000 the Navy took delivery of the first of a proposed three Advanced SEAL Delivery Systems (ASDS). At over $250 million a copy, the first 65-foot ASDS was delivered to SEAL Delivery Team ONE at Pearl Harbor, Hawaii, to begin several months of rigorous deepwater testing.

The ASDS was designed and developed by a team drawn from Northrop Grumman Oceanic & Naval Systems, NAVSEA, Deep Submergence, and USSOCOM. Multi-mission capable, the ASDS is more like a space shuttle than just a wet SDV, and has two pilots, one officer from COMSUB and one from SEALs. To be selected for the ASDS program, SEALs must be post-platoon commander Lieutenants who are SDV qualified and have had extensive experience in conducting submarine operations.

The ASDS Pilot training program is still in its infancy, but one hurdle the officers from the submarine service have to overcome is dive school. All ASDS pilots are required to attend a special five-week program at Navy Dive School get their diving certifications and learn more about diving physiology, diving related injuries, and chamber operations. This can be difficult for an officer coming from the sub command where physical fitness requirements are not up to the standards for dive school.

Actually flying the ASDS is reportedly much easier for the sub officers since they learned many of the necessary skills as a junior submarine officer. A joystick is used to control the vehicle and computer screens supply all the necessary data on ballast and attitude. The ASDS can also be programmed to fly a course "almost by itself" by entering the necessary data and waypoints.

This manned, dry interior, battery-powered vehicle provides extended range, greater speed and payload, and habitability for the crew and a team of SEALs. The ASDS can be transported to its designated area of operation by a specially configured submarine, and is also air transportable by either C-5 Galaxy or C-17 Globemaster aircraft.

Submarines are converted with latching pylons and a hatch in order to host the ASDS for transport to mission areas. Once the host submarine is on station, the ASDS disconnects, navigates into shallow waters closer to the objective, and then anchors on the bottom. The SEALs can then deploy into the water and make the final approach swim to their target. On prolonged operations, the SEALs can use the ASDS as an underwater safe-haven where they can rest-up and retool for the next mission.

Once the mission is completed and the SOF team is retrieved, the ASDS navigates back to the host submarine and re-attaches using special locking mechanisms. Once the ASDS is properly mated to the host sub, personnel and equipment can be transferred, similar to current practice with a Deep Submergence Rescue Vehicle (DSRV).

In May, 2002, ASDS Boat 1 successfully completed 12 separate docking scenarios with the primary host simulator. The simulator is a replica of the topside of a submarine with latching mechanisms, located on the ocean floor off the coast of Hawaii. Since December of last year, Boat 1 has also completed a number of tests while attached to an operational submarine.

In September, 2002, ASDS Boat 1 successfully completed multiple launch and recovery docking scenarios with the USS Greeneville (SSN 772). The successive dockings over a several day period validated the capability of the system to operate in the undersea environment.[4]

In June, 2003, the Deep Submergence Systems Program and the ASDS program manager for NAVSEA signed the official document that delivered the ASDS into the hands of the Navy.

"This first-of-its-kind system provides a new level of operational capability to SEAL forces in high-threat areas," said Capt. Fallone. "The delivery of ASDS marks a major milestone in ensuring that our Naval forces have the most technologically advanced equipment for today's critical missions."

The teams and pilots that currently support the ASDS program are developing new tactics and techniques and redefining what may become the norm for submarine-launched SOF operations for the next two decades. There is no doubt that SEALs transported in a dry sub will arrive on target better prepared for their mission than if they had just completed a several-hour transit in a wet SDV.

An ASDS submarine is designed to carry Navy SEALs.

Maintenance and training facility for the ASDS.

ENDNOTES

1   Naval Forces Under the Sea proceedings. Presentation by Captain Norman Olson, USN (Ret), who served in numerous commands in Naval Special Warfare

2   Author's conversation with Commander Roger Herbert at SDVT2

3   Dry Deck Shelters—Deploying Special Operations Forces from Submarines, by Steve Southard, NAVSEA's Deckplate Jan-Feb 1999

4   Navy and Northrop press release

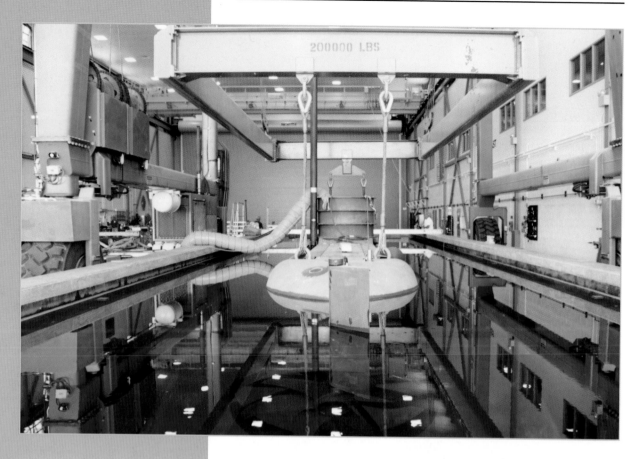

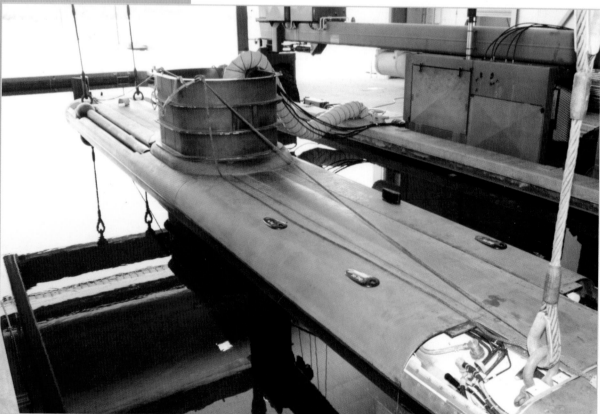

ASDS Training Facility
Pearl Harbor, Hawaii

Full-face mask (FFM).

*Servicing the MK16
at the SDV school.*

MK16 with Heads-up display.

MK16 used on SDV operations.

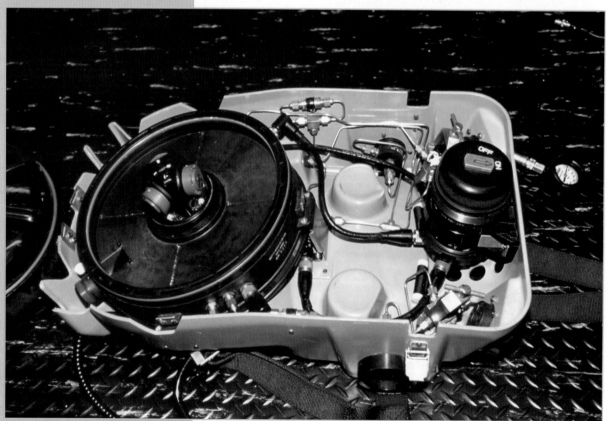

*MK16 minus the scrubber and
gas cylinders.*

MK16 helium and oxygen cylinders.

*Dive control for the DDS and
SDV operations.*

U.S. Marine
Combatant
Divers

16

USMC

"A FEW GOOD MEN"

The reconnaissance missions of United States Marines take them to areas of operation where they are expected to infiltrate hostile territory to conduct reconnaissance or other direct action combat missions. Often the Reconnaissance Marine must enter these objectives underwater in order to achieve a clandestine approach and increase the probability for mission success.

To prepare Marines for this mission, the US Marine Corps Combatant Diver Course was designed at the Naval Diving & Salvage Training Center, Panama City, Florida, in conjunction with the Marine Corps Combat Development Command, Quantico, Virginia. The MCD course is very much designed by Marines and run by Marines for the Marines.

The purpose of the course is to provide the Marines with the best possible underwater combat swim training available, and in so doing maintain their traditions of the best-trained fighting force in the world.

The Combatant Diver Course develops highly confident and capable Recon Marines, schooled in the most current tactical doctrines and equipment, and ready to conduct an underwater infiltration and exfiltration as required by a mission commander.

THE COMBATANT DIVER COURSE

Amphibious Reconnaissance is a coastal landing conducted by reconnaissance elements for the purpose of securing information that will aid in mission planning. This task normally requires stealth rather than force of arms, and is usually followed by an equally stealthily planned withdrawal. When conducted underwater, the success of this insertion or extraction depends greatly on the individual Marine and the reconnaissance team's abilities to negotiate long distances in the water with the equipment organic to their respective commands and the Marine Corps Expeditionary Units – Special Operations Capable (MEU-SOC).[1]

Reconnaissance platoons that operate in small teams with minimum support for extended periods of time recognize the importance of having well-trained, capable individuals. The Combatant Diver Course meets this requirement by providing diver training through academics, extensive physical training, pool familiarization dives, open water surface swims, and underwater infiltration swims with approximately 60% of the open water diving conducted at night.

At the end of the course the students are assigned mission profiles where they are required to infiltrate underwater into their objective areas. These missions may include MEU (SOC) Maritime Special Purpose Force (MSPF) type reconnaissance or direct action missions.

The Combatant Diver Course is 35 training days in length and divided into four modules of training: Physical Conditioning, Combat Diver Principles & Fundamentals, USMC Open Circuit Diving Equipment & Operations, and USMC Closed Circuit Diving Equipment & Operations. Upon successful completion of the training, students are certified by the US Navy and the Marine Corps as USMC Combatant Divers.

But getting to that final graduation is no easy task. In fact, the MCD course is one of the most physically demanding at NDSTC.

MK25 CCBA.

Physical training is conducted twice daily. Morning PT consists of a 60-minute period of calisthenics, running, and/or swimming, with increasing difficulty imposed as the weeks progress. The students participate in three to seven mile timed runs. Tactical surface swims are conducted daily, with distances increasing from 500 yards to 10,000 yards, often conducted with combat equipment, including rifles, load bearing vests, and simulated ammunition loads.

After academic fundamentals and open-circuit SCUBA training, Marines move into the focus of the course, closed-circuit diving operations. This phase of training includes classroom instruction, pool training, compass swims, advanced navigation techniques, and underwater infiltration and exfiltration dives.

To bring an element of reality to the training, students function as combatant diver team members during underwater infiltration and exfiltration swims with combat equipment. Using a combat rubber raiding craft (CRRC) as the delivery vehicle, the students are trained to perform an over the horizon (OTH) turtle-back swim on the surface, immediately followed by a closed-circuit underwater infiltration.

The end of training is marked with the class, in four to eight man reconnaissance teams, executing a field training exercise that requires them to infiltrate in surface and sub-surface mode, move to and conduct assigned missions on land, and extract from their assigned objective area without being observed or compromised.

The end result of the course is a Marine who is an effective and capable Combatant Diver with the proven ability to overcome the rigorous mental and physical challenges imposed on the individual during an underwater infiltration in amphibious operations. With that designator, the Landing Force Commander can be confident that he has

Recon divers going through pre-deployment diving refresher program.

competent, well-trained, physically capable Reconnaissance Marines who are prepared to execute any mission requiring an underwater projection of power into the tactical arena.

AFTER DIVE SCHOOL

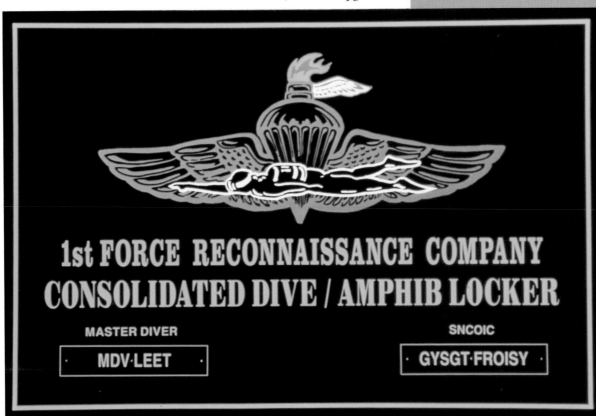

Marine Recon Diver

Once a Recon Marine has completed combat swimmer training at NDSTC, he will be assigned to, or return to, his post with Marine Reconnaissance or a Force Reconnaissance platoon. From there training will continue at the company and platoon level.

To meet the operational requirements of the Battalion Commander to whom they will be attached, Recon Marines train constantly in preparation for their next overseas deployment, often referred to as "float."

In a perfect world, Force Recon Marines will run a two-year training cycle, beginning with six months of individual schools where they will attend a variety of specialized training such as military freefall, diving, sniper, communications, etc. This is followed by six months of platoon training where they practice all their skills as a cohesive fighting unit. It is at this point in their training cycle that they will get recurrent training with their rebreathers and combat swimming tactics and techniques.

Platoon training is a series of pre-scheduled two-week training cycles, including evolutions in combat communications, weapons & tactics,

(Continued pg 262)

**1st FORCE RECONNAISSANCE COMPANY
CONSOLIDATED DIVE / AMPHIB LOCKER**

MASTER DIVER

· MDV·LEET ·

SNCOIC

· GYSGT·FROISY ·

Sign at the Camp Pendleton Recon Diving and Amphibious Operations Center (2001).

Pre-dive checks.

Waterproof communication headset for MBITR radio.

Both the company commander and executive officer train alongside their recon Marines.

Practicing helo-casts.

M249 Squad automatic weapon (SAW)—5.56mm.

Daytime dive ops training.

*Loaded out for night patrol
and reconaissance training.*

"Quick - Silent - Deadly" the Recon motto.

amphibious boat operations, combat diving, mountain warfare, and high altitude freefall parachute jumping.

For the Force Recon platoons assigned to 1st Force Recon Company at Camp Pendleton, the two-week dive package is supported by the Company Dive Locker (CDL). Located near the base marina, CDL has both an Amphibious Section and a Dive Section staffed by Recon instructors and ten Navy-trained divers (4 Navy/6 USMC) who serve primarily as observers and evaluators for the Recon Marines. The Recon platoon commanders plan and run their own training evolutions while the Navy divers serve as subject-matter experts on diving and diving equipment, and will offer advice on new diving techniques or changes in operational procedure.

As with most military skill-sets, combat swimming is a perishable skill, especially when it must be done at night, in dark unfamiliar waters. This two weeks of intense instruction and training exercises is designed to revisit all the skills that the Marines learned at the Combatant Diver course and then up-date them with current operational tactics and techniques.

Finally, after a year of individual and platoon training, the Recon platoon will "chop to the MEU" where they will go through an additional six months of pre-deployment training with the Marine Corps' Special Operations Training Group (SOTG). At the completion of MEU spin-ups, the Recon platoon will load up all their equipment, and "go on float" for the next six months. However, with the current war on terrorism and military commitment to OEF and OIF, training cycles are often condensed and deployments can stretch to eight or nine months.

Portable recompression chamber in the USMC Recon Company dive locker.

Mountain warfare training,
September 2001.

MWTC, 2001.

GOING TO WAR

The very purpose of the Marine Expeditionary Unit (MEU) is to serve as a forward deployed asset of US foreign policy, what is commonly referred to as force projection.

At any given time, MEUs are pre-positioned at hotspots around the globe ready for immediate deployment. The MEU-SOC (Special Operations Capable) is structured as a fully self-sufficient fighting force including a Battalion Landing Team (BLT), Marine Corps Light Armor & Artillery, and Marine Corps Aircraft & Pilots.

The reinforced Battalion Landing Team, made up of roughly 54 officers and 1,178 enlisted, fits into the limited space aboard a 3-ship Amphibious Ready Group (ARG). This also includes the Command Element and its various reconnaissance assets — Force Recon, Battalion

Training wing Gunny Sergeant videoing dive training for post-exercise debrief.

Reconnaissance, a Scout-Sniper platoon, and a contingent of SEALs.

Battalion Recon is the reconnaissance asset of the Battalion Commander and operates up to and just past the forward edge of the battle area. They serve as the tactical commander's eyes and ears, reporting on enemy strength, activity, location, and movement.

Force Recon is more of a strategic intelligence asset tasked with pushing further into hostile territory, up to 300 miles on deep reconnaissance missions, to collect information and intelligence on terrain, weather, suitable landing zones (LZ), and enemy disposition and activity. In addition, Recon Marines are also tasked with a variety of special operations Direct Action missions when teamed up with SEALs and snipers as a Maritime Special Purpose Force (MSPF). It is primarily the Recon Marines, SEALs, and Snipers that give the MEU its special operations capabilities.

So wherever the battalion goes, the Recon Marines are sure to be there first. And since Marines are traditionally a littoral fighting force, this often requires the use of combat diving techniques for sub-surface, covert approaches used in over-the-beach operations. A typical mission may have recon divers swimming into a hostile coastal region, or up a river deep within enemy controlled territory, to scout potential beach landing sites, identify natural or man-made obstacles, report on enemy defenses, or secure helicopter landing zones (HLZ). Recon Marines are also trained to direct naval gunfire to destroy enemy defenses, and coordinate close air support (CAS) for the battalion landing teams.

The variety and complexity of the missions required of Recon Marines make them one of the most highly trained groups in the Marine Corps, but they are still a very small component of the over-all Marine Corps force structure. However, it is this small size, dictated by both mission and rigorous selection, that makes them the elite in an organization that considers all Marines to be special. Recon Marines epitomize the Marine Corps recruiting slogan "…looking for a Few Good Men." When you only have a few lightly armed men going in harms way, they must all be good, and Marine Recon are the very best of that few.

ENDNOTES

1   Course description from MCD dive locker, NDSTC

Latest version of the USMC K-bar.

U.S. Navy Combat Camera Divers

17

US Navy Combat Camera (COMCAM) units do exactly as their name states—they go into combat with cameras. Their primary mission is to provide the National Command Authority (NCA), the Chairman of the Joint Chiefs of Staff (JCS), the Navy, and the Unified Combatant Commands with imagery that will support planning and operations during international crises, military exercises, and wartime operations.

Combat Camera personnel use video and still photography to gather images of intelligence value in forward operating areas, such as in Afghanistan and Iraq. Their number one priority is to capture images of intelligence and operational value to the theater commander, and the immediate transmission of this often time-sensitive imagery back to the Pentagon for briefing to the Joint Chiefs of Staff.

In addition to the more sensitive images for command intelligence, additional images and video footage are released to the media for news and documentary distribution, but only after proper authority review. Much of this imagery is also utilized by other commands and services for training.

COMCAM COMMANDS

The US Navy has two COMCAM units: Fleet Combat Camera Atlantic (FCCA), based in Norfolk, VA, and Fleet Combat Camera Group Pacific, located in San Diego, CA—but as of 2004, only FCCA has assigned Navy-trained divers capable of documenting underwater operations and training.

FCCA Mission Statement is a visual information acquisition unit, providing photographic documentation covering air, sea, and ground operations of armed forces engaged in combat, combat support operations, humanitarian efforts, scientific research, and related peacetime activities such as exercises and war games. Additionally, supporting Combat Operations, Operational Requirements, and Technical Evaluations.[1]

COMBAT CAMERA DIVERS

FCCA maintains the only dive-capable Combat Camera unit within the Department of Defense. In addition to numerous combat missions, this rather unique dive locker has provided Combat Camera divers to several air disasters, including the Swissair 111 crash, the Egypt Air crash, and the recovery of John F. Kennedy Jr.'s small plane off Cape Cod.

Combat Camera divers are fully trained US Navy divers, with FCCA billeted for three 1st Class divers and two 2nd Class divers, qualifying them to dive surface-supplied with the MK 21. This was the case on the *Monitor* project, where PHC (SW/DV) Andy McKaskle and his Combat Camera divers were descending to 240 feet on mixed-gas to document the MDSU-2 divers working and the recovery of critical components of the historic Civil War ironclad gunboat.

(Continued pg 276)

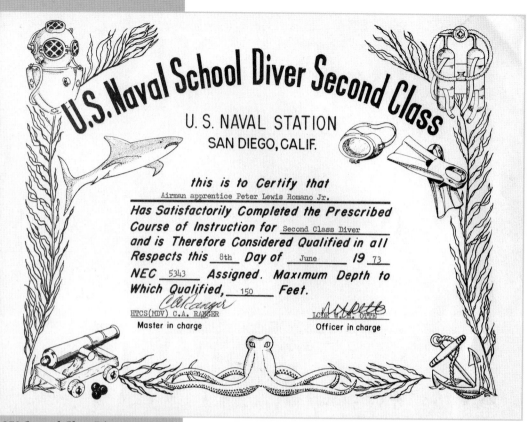

1973 Second Class Diver Certificate for combat camera group diver Pete Romano.

CCG divers Romano (L) and Kulu (R) in both images (circa 1974).

*Second Class Dive School,
San Diego, CA (1975).*

32nd Street, San Diego (1975)

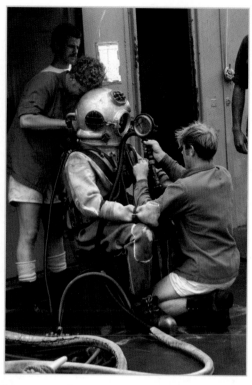

*Combat camera group
documented Navy divers
training in 1975.*

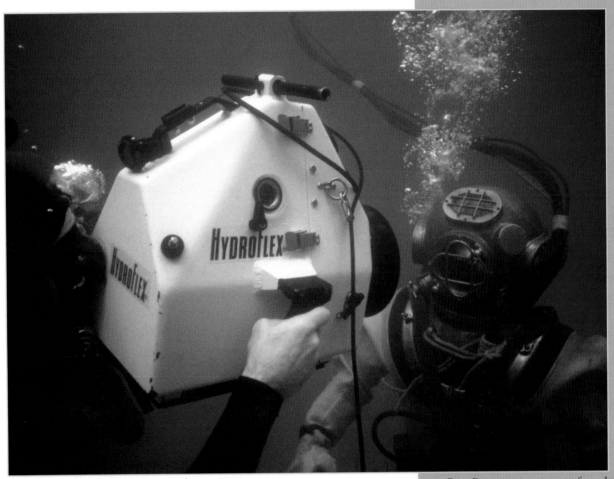

Pete Romano went on to found Hydroflex—the foremost underwater camera and lighting company in the film industry. Pete is seen here filming "Men of Honor."

Combat camera diver with the early Milliken 16mm camera in a Rebikoff housing. (Anacap 1975).

Author training with the Hydroflex 35mm deep housing and camera system.

U.S. Navy combat camera diver
with Amphibico housing and
digital video.

PHC (SW/DV Andy McKaskle on
the Monitor Project (2001).

CDU diver prepares a lightweight digital camera for an inspection dive.

Combat camera divers documenting the Ehime Maru *recovery project.*

*Combat camera diving mixed gas
on the* Monitor *Project*

*Photographers use a variety of film
and digital cameras.*

*First female Navy scuba
diver (1974).*

When filming on or under the water, Combat Camera divers use a selection of state-of-the-art digital video systems and cameras. This move to digital has also facilitated their capabilities in streaming these images around the globe, back to command, or the Joint Combat Camera Center (JCCC) in Washington, DC.

Combat Camera personnel are fortunate to have state-of-the-art camera and video equipment. On the *Monitor* project, the Combat Camera divers were using high-end Nikon digital still cameras and Sony video systems, all with expensive wide angle lens and compatible underwater housings.

In addition to the significant contributions of PHC (SW/DV) Andrew McKaskle, who has captured so many fine images of Navy diving, the following Navy combat cameramen and photographers also contributed images to this book.

Petty Officer Diver Eric Lippman, Chief Photographer (DV) Mark M. Reinhard, PH2 Isaac Merriman, Senior Chief Photographer Terry Cosgrove, and PHC (SW/NAC) Spike Call. Photographer's Mates First Class Jim Hampshire, David S. Tucker, Eric J. Tilford, Robert Palmares, David C. Lloyd, Michael J. Rinaldi, and Auguest C. Sigur. PH2 (AW) Brain McFadden, PH2's (AW/NAC) Keith DeVinney, Felix Garza Jr., and Matthew J. Magee. PH3's Kris White, Timothy Lago, Joshua L. Pritekel, and Lolita D. Swain. PH Airmen Caroline Hammonds and Michael Hursey, and Journalist Mates Tyler A. Swartz and Jason E. Miller.

To those whose images appear in this book but have not been mentioned, my apologies and thanks.

ENDNOTES
1   FCCA mission statement

Deep
Submergence &
Submarine Rescue

The US NAVY maintains a number of deep recovery capabilities, several of which are intended for submarine rescue, that do not fall strictly into the realm of diving since they are either unmanned or one-atmosphere vehicles. Although pilots and operators descend to considerable depths in these rescue vehicles, they are hydronauts but not divers, since they are not physically under pressure, do not get wet, and can return to the surface without the need for decompression. However, the commands that operate deep one-atmosphere suits and ROVs also have Navy divers to assist with the launch and recovery of these high-tech vehicles.

Post-dive wash down.

In addition to submarine rescue, Deep Submergence becomes involved in deep salvage and recovery operations when the target is deeper than 300 feet—the limit of surface-supplied mixed-gas Navy divers. In 2001, Deep Submergence was involved in the recovery of the *Ehime Maru* from 2000 fsw off Hawaii, and back in 1966 was instrumental in the search and successful recovery of a hydrogen bomb lost off the coast of Spain in 2850 feet.

SUBMARINE DEVELOPMENT SQUADRON FIVE

Mission Statement: "(To be the) world leader in undersea operations through development of tomorrow's technology and tactics, providing United States Submariners with the best off-hull sensor, rescue, and arctic capabilities while conducting challenging global deployments in support of national interests."[1]

Submarine Development Squadron Five was established in 1967, originally as Submarine Development Group ONE, as the operational focal point for Navy Deep Submergence, Submarine Rescue, Ocean Engineering, and Research and Development Programs. SUBDEVRON FIVE is responsible within the submarine force for tactical development in the areas of escape, rescue, diving, unmanned underwater vehicles, Naval Special Warfare, and Arctic operability. This includes developing and testing new tactics and systems for incorporation and dissemination within the submarine force.

The command supports submarine and diving assets at Naval Submarine Base, San Diego, CA, and Bangor, WA, which include diesel and nuclear-powered research submarines, and deep submergence rescue vehicles (DSRV) as part of the Deep Submergence Unit.

DSRV and ROV support ship Kelly Choust.

Scorpio deep remote operated vehicle (ROV). Note articulate arms and thrusters.

Scorpio aboard the Kelly Choust.

Scorpio ROV.

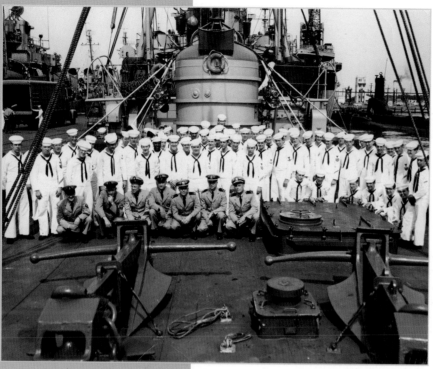

USS Skylark ASR 20 in Norfolk, Virginia, 1957. Rescue bell in center, mooring anchors in foreground.

SUBMARINE RESCUE

Vice Admiral Charles (Swede) Momsen, US Navy Diving and Submarine Pioneer, was a major contributor to diving research, submarine rescue, diving equipment development, deep diving oper-ations, and operations with military submarines. During his long and distinguished career in the US Navy, he helped develop the famous submarine escape device known as the Momsen Lung.

USS Wandank *(AT26) and USS* Falcon *(ASR2) moored over the sunken* Squalus *during rescue operations in May of 1939. The McCann Rescue Chamber is visible on* Falcon's *afterdeck.*

Diving gang on the USS Fulton, *New London, Connecticut, 1965.*

Crewman A.L. Rosenkotter of US V-5 (SC 1) demonstrates the use of the submarine's after escape hatch and the emergency escape "lung" during V-5's trials in July of 1930.

Several variations of the "Momsen Lung" apparatus. Left to right: TM1(DV) Edward Kalinowski in an experimental metal canister, SF1(DV) John Iben in an experimental rubber canister, and LT Charles Momsen in a circular tube around shoulders, March, 1928.

Vice Admiral Charles B. Momsen, USN (1896–1967).

USS Momsen.

ADS 2000 support team at work.

*DSRV piggybacking on
a mother submarine.*

DEEP SUBMERGENCE UNIT

Deep Submergence Unit (DSU) was established in 1989 and is home of the Navy's manned and unmanned deep diving submersibles. Located at Naval Air Station North Island (NASNI) in San Diego are Deep Submergence Rescue Vehicles (DSRV) MYSTIC and AVALON, a variety of unmanned Remotely Operated Vehicles (ROV), and Submarine Rescue Chambers (SRC).

DSU was originally chartered as Submarine Rescue Unit following the loss of USS *Thresher* (SSN 593), and received DSRV-1 MYSTIC in 1971 and DSRV-2 AVALON in 1972, with a mandate to maintain the capability to locate a disabled submarine, accomplish reliable personnel escape and rescue, and optimize survival possibilities in a bottomed submarine.[2]

MYSTIC and AVALON are capable of diving to 5,000 feet and are maintained in a high state of readiness with one vehicle always in standby status. In an emergency, the Ready Rescue Vehicle will load into a US Air Force C-5 aircraft at NAS North Island, fly to a location near the disabled submarine, load onto a specially configured "mother submarine" (MOSUB), and be transported "piggy back" to the downed submarine. The DSRV has two pilots, two rescue personnel, and can accommodate 24 passengers. The DSRV also has an alternate mission configuration to conduct deep ocean search and recovery operations.

Unmanned Vehicles Detachment operates side-looking sonar systems (SILOS) and state-of-the-art deep ocean ROVs, including two Super SCORPIO Tethered Unmanned Work Vehicle Systems. These advanced vehicles are operated at the end of a tether, controlled from a surface support ship, and have significant recovery capabilities. Working to depths of 5,000 feet, UMVs are capable of submerged operations for extended periods and were called into service on the TWA crash and the recovery of the *Ehime Maru*. In recent years, the Detachment has been responsible for the recovery of over 100 million dollars worth of military and civilian hardware.

The Unmanned Undersea Vehicle Detachment is responsible for the operation and maintenance of Submarine Launched Unmanned Undersea Vehicle (UUV) systems. Detachment personnel deploy on board submarine platforms in support of Navy UUV intelligence collection requirements. The Detachment also participated in development and testing of the Navy's new Mine Reconnaissance UUV system (AN/BLQ-11).

Diving Systems Support Detachment (DSSD) consists of Navy deep-sea divers and Submarine Rescue Chambers that provide world-wide submarine rescue capability to depths of 850 feet. DSSD also performs operational developmental testing of advanced diving systems such as the Atmosphere Diving Suit (ADS) in preparation for fleet acceptance.

ENDNOTES

1   SUBDEVRON 5 web page
2   DSU web page

ADS 2000 testing.

DSRV aboard a support ship.

*ADS 2000 launch and
recovery frame.*

Hanging out in a one-atmosphere diving suit.

DSRV is air transportable in a C-5 Galaxy.

DSRV being off-loaded.

*DSRV being loaded aboard a
mother submarine (MOSUB).*

DSRV Chiyoda *dives from mother ship JDS* Chiyoda *(1999).*

Deep Saturation Diving

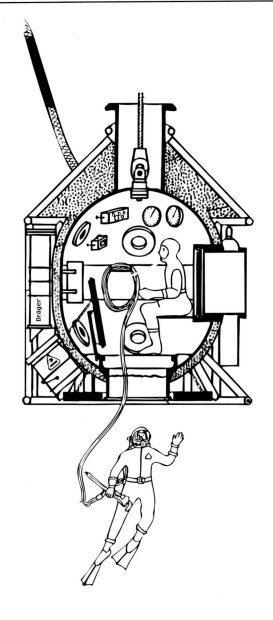

nlike deep submergence, where operators are encapsulated in heated one-atmosphere comfort, the deep diving mixed gas diver is required to drop down to considerable depth, 200–1000 feet, and deal with the cold and extreme pressure. Deep diving, even with relatively short bottom times, also carries a heavy decompression penalty for the divers, requiring that they make numerous in-water decompression stops before surfacing. If diving on Surface Decompression Tables using Oxygen (SUR-D O$_2$), the diver will then have to spend additional time in the recompression chamber breathing 100% oxygen, or risk a severe case of the bends (DCS).

Decompression sickness is a direct result of gases dissolved in the diver's body, but it was found in experimental dives that the diver became saturated with gas after 12 hours. After that, the diver's decompression time would remain the same, immaterial of the length of time under pressure. This opened the door for saturation diving where the divers were kept under pressure for 20–30 days, and work time on the bottom became limited only by physical endurance.

Using this form of diving, divers are stored in the saturation system, which is a series of large chambers and transfer locks, kept at a pressure slightly less than the targeted working depth. Two-man dive teams are then transferred to and from the dive site in pressurized personnel transfer capsules (PTC), more commonly called a diving bell. When the external pressure in the water equals the internal pressure in the bell, the doors pop open, allowing the divers to exit the bell and work.

While one diver remains in the bell to tend the umbilical, the other diver is able to work for up to four hours in the water. At the end of four hours the divers switch out, for a total of eight hours productive dive time. The bell is then recovered to the surface, locked onto the system, and the dive teams switch out. In this manner, three 2-man teams can dive 24 hours a day, weather permitting.

At the end of their period of saturation, 20–30 days, the divers are brought back to the surface in a slow and controlled bleed-off of pressure from the chambers. It would take four days of decompression to bring divers back from a depth of four hundred feet and a week from 600 feet.

Saturation diver.

HISTORY OF SATURATION DIVING

The US Navy's involvement in deep air diving can be traced back to the 1915 salvage of the USS *F-4*, when the divers also realized the limitations of deep air diving. Nitrogen narcosis would degrade the divers' performance at depths greater than 200 feet, and the required decompression after a working dive was significant.

Deep mixed-gas diving became practical with the 500-foot dive performed at NEDU in 1937 and the subsequent recovery of the USS *Squalus* from 243 feet in 1939. This solved the nitrogen narcosis problem but not the long in-water decompression. These deep dives graphically demonstrated that working at depth exposed the diver to considerable

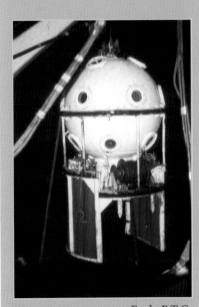

Early P.T.C.

P.T.C. at NEDU from the
ASR-21 Pigeon.

MK 21 Air/Mixed gas hat.

personal risk, hypothermia, and a long, uncomfortable decompression. It was also realized that it might be possible to use a diving bell to transfer the diver to and from the bottom, adding both safety and comfort for the dive team.

This thinking was put into practice with the Man-in-the-Sea project in 1962 and the first Sealab experiments in 1964. SEALAB I put divers to 192 fsw for 10 days off Bermuda; then in 1965, SEALAB II put three dive teams to 205 fsw for 10–16 days each in the La Jolla Canyon off Scripps Institute of Oceanography in California.

The follow-on seafloor experiment, SEALAB III, was planned for 610 fsw. Divers were to use semi-closed mixed-gas rigs, with five teams of 8 divers spending 12 days on the bottom. The divers were to be tasked with testing new salvage techniques, along with performing oceanographic and fishery studies. This was a joint military and civilian program including military divers from the US, UK, Canada, and Australia.

This huge undertaking required not only extensive development and testing of equipment but also assessment of human tolerance to high-pressure environments. To prepare for SEALAB III, 28 helium-oxygen saturation dives were performed between 1965 and 1968 at the Navy Experimental Diving Unit (NEDU) to depths of 825 fsw.

In 1968, a record-breaking excursion dive to 1,025 fsw from a saturation depth of 825 fsw was performed at NEDU. The culmination of this series of dives was a 1,000 fsw, 3-day saturation dive conducted jointly by the US Navy and Duke University in the hyperbaric chambers at Duke. This was the first time man had been saturated at 1,000 fsw. The SEALAB III preparation experiments showed that divers could perform useful work at pressures up to 31 atmospheres and could be returned to normal pressure without harm.

Unfortunately, SEALAB III was to end in disaster in the first days of diving. On February 17,1969, SEALAB III was terminated with the death of diver Berry Cannon at over 600 feet. The investigation revealed that he had been given a MK IX diving rig with no CO_2 absorbent and was overcome by the carbon dioxide build-up in the system.[1]

However, by the end of SEALAB III the Navy had already proven that saturation diving could be considered a viable operational capability.

DEEP DIVING SYSTEMS

Even though SEALAB was finished, the Navy continued to develop safer and more efficient ways to support divers at depth. Much of this work focused on deep diving systems (DDS) that could be mated to submersible decompression systems (SDS).

In 1967 the first DDS & SDS-450 deep diving system was placed in Fleet Service by Harbor Clearance Unit One but was only used for non-saturation dives. Then in 1968 the MK-2 Mod 0 Deep Diving System was developed and put aboard the *Elk River* (IX-501) to support SEALAB III. Commissioned in 1945, the *Elk River* was originally built as a Landing Ship, Medium Rocket (LSMR-501) but was later reconfigured with a moon-pool to support diving operations.

In 1970 the DDS MK-1 Deep Diving System came into service, and in October made a world record open-sea dive to 850 feet. The DDS MK-1 was a transportable system with a decompression chamber and personnel transfer capsule (PTC).

At this time, diving equipment was also being developed that would better suit the needs of the divers working out of diving bells. The MK-10 closed-circuit mixed-gas diving system was designed to be used for PTC lock-outs to 1500 fsw, and the MK-11 semi-closed circuit mixed-gas system consisted of a helmet and re-circulating backpack designed for use to 850 fsw.

In 1972 the DDS MK-2 MOD 0 set the in-water depth record of 1,010 fsw. Unlike the MK-1, which was a

P.T.C. launch.

SEALAB I.

transportable system, the DDS MK-2 was designed for installation only on specially configured rescue and salvage ships and barges.

To meet the needs of the fleet, two diving systems were installed on ASR class submarine rescue vessels—one port and one starboard. Commissioned in 1973, ASR-21 *Pigeon* and ASR-22 *Ortolan* were equipped as DSRV, submarine rescue, and saturation diving support platforms capable of supporting diving operations to 850 feet. *Pigeon*, working out of San Diego, and *Ortolan* out of Norfolk, were ideally suited to diving operations, with wide catamaran-design hulls that offered both stability and ample deck space for work.

In 1975 divers using the MK 1 DDS descended to 1,148 fsw; then in 1976 the Navy approved the MK-1 Mod 0 Light-weight, Mixed-Gas Diving Outfit for dives to 300 fsw on helium-oxygen.

Capt. MSC Walter Mazzone USNR involved from Genesis through SEALAB III.

Capt. George Foote Bond MC, SEALAB topside control and Deputy Medical Affairs. Capt. Bond is considered the father of saturation diving.

The USS *Jimmy Carter*, set to join the nation's submarine fleet in year 2005, was designed to have some special capabilities that were the results of Sea Lab III program. SEALAB III was missioned (charged) to develop extreme depth skills during the President Nixon administration, specifically the ability to tap undersea cables and eavesdrop on the communications passing through them. The USS *Jimmy Carter*, the third and last of the Seawolf class of attack subs, is at a cost of over 3.2 billion dollars. The previous submarine that performed the mission, the USS *Parche*, was retired in 2004. The new sub is designed to house technicians and diving capabilities to perform the cable-tapping and other secret missions. The hull section is 100 feet longer than the other two subs in the Seawolf class, a total length of 453 feet, and will provide berths for up to 50 special operations troops, like the US Navy SEALS. A tremendous amount of credit is attributed to the men and senior officers involved in the SEALAB III project.

CDR. Jackson M. Tomsky, USN, known as Blackjack, head of the Ocean Engineering Branch of Deep Submergence Systems and Commander for the SEALAB III operation.

26 August 1965: 1,000 yards west of the Scripps Institute of Oceanography pier, SEALAB II being prepared to descend 205 feet to the sea floor, with the Berkone in support.

February 1969, off San Clemente Island: SEALAB III being prepared for its 610-foot descent commencing at 4:36 p.m., 15 February, at a descent rate of 4 feet per minute.

September 1965: Captain Bond and Captain Mazzone make a brief 205-foot mixed-gas scuba dive to visit SEALAB and team II. From left to right: Howard Buckner, Chief Steelworker (DV) USN, Mazzone, and Bond.

SEALAB III, Team I Aquanats:
From left to right kneeling: Berry
Cannon, civilian; Jay Meyers,
Machinist's Mate Second Class,
USN; LCDR James Vorosmarti Jr.,
MC, USN; Richard Cooper,
civilian. From left to right
standing: George Dowling, civilian;
Richard Blackburn, Aviation
Ordnanceman First Class, USN;
Warrant Officer Robert Barth,
USN, Team Leader; John Reaves,
Photographer's Mate First Class,
USN (replacement for Lt. Laurence
Bussey); and Richard Bird,
Engineman First Class, USN.

Aquanat Berry Cannon.

The MK 1 Deep Diving System went out of service in 1977, but the MK-2 Mod 1 DDS continued in service to support two 4-man saturation teams for long periods at a normal operating depth capability of 950 feet.

The US Navy and NEDU had been responsible for much of the research and development of saturation diving tables, and by the seventies saturation diving had become common in commercial oilfield diving (the author made his first deep saturation dive in 1977). Research continued at NEDU, and in 1979 divers completed a 37-day saturation dive to 1800 fsw in the Ocean Simulator Facility (OSF). Unfortunately, by the late eighties the Navy was replacing shipboard saturation diving with DSRV and ROV operations.

While diving operations continued on the *Pigeon* and *Ortolan*, by the mid-eighties the *Elk River* was being used as a Saturation Diving School. However, funding was becoming tight, and it was difficult to keep these expensive diving systems operating and up to strict Navy certification.

Then came the end of the Cold War. In 1989 the Iron Curtain came down, along with the Berlin Wall, and the funding for saturation diving operations dried up. The *Pigeon* was decommissioned in 1992, the *Ortolan* in 1995, and *Elk River* went into mothballs, to be stricken from the record in 1999 and was sunk in gunnery practice in 2001.

With the development of the DSRV and deep ROV capabilities, the Navy could no longer support the costs associated with deep saturation diving for salvage and submarine rescue. Much to the dismay of the Navy diving community, this, sadly, marked the end of shipboard saturation systems in the US Navy.

As of this writing, Italian, Swedish, and Romanian navies currently have saturation diving capabilities, but the US Navy still does not own a mobile or shipboard sat system. Saturation diving and research continues in the Ocean Simulator at NEDU, and to date the Navy has over one hundred active saturation divers, but saturation diving systems have been absent from the surface fleet and submarine rescue ships since the end of the Cold War.

SATURATION ON THE *MONITOR* PROJECT

With the Navy's involvement in the *Monitor* project, it became evident that the long-duration deep dives required could be done with greater safety and efficiency with the use of a saturation system and diving bell. Surface-supplied divers, supported from the surface, had only 20–30 minutes of useable bottom time at 240 feet, followed by in-water decompression stops and a lengthy decompression in the chamber breathing oxygen.

Saturation divers, on the other hand, would be able to spend three or four hours working on the bottom with each dive, without having to do any decompression until the end of their saturation period. This was both safer and more efficient — but not cheap.

The first hurdle to overcome was the fact that the Navy no longer maintained saturation diving systems, but they did have contracts with a number of civilian diving companies that owned sat systems. But again, hiring one would not be cheap.

So the second hurdle became money. Without funding, the Navy would not have been able to deploy a saturation diving system on the *Monitor* project — but thanks to the efforts of Senator Warren of Virginia and funding from the DOD Legacy Program, 00C was able to move forward with the project. From SUPSALV, Master Diver Young, Rob Warren, and the 00C4 team undertook an exhaustive evaluation of the civilian saturation system to be used.

Another major player in making the use of saturation diving a reality was OPNAV N773, Navy-speak for the Deep Submergence Submarine Warfare Division. This command is responsible for the employment of deep submergence vehicles, unmanned undersea vehicles, and diver systems, as well as the conduct of submarine search and rescue.

Global Diving already held contracts to support a variety of US Navy diving projects, so they were the logical source for a saturation system. Global supplied a 1500-foot saturation system, consisting of a diving bell and pressurized living quarters, along with support personnel to train and assist the Navy divers.

In saturation diving, multiple 2-man dive teams live in the deck chambers, and when ready to dive, two divers climb into the diving bell through a transfer lock and seal the doors. The diving bell is then unlocked from the chambers and lowered into the water to transport the divers to the sea floor. When the pressure in the water equals the pressure inside the bell, the lower hatch can be opened.

One diver wearing a hot water suit and helmet, and trailing an umbilical, then drops into the water to go to work. At the end of his 3–4 hour dive he returns to the bell and switches out with the other diver.

At the end of the dive, and when both divers are safely back in the bell, the doors are sealed and the bell is brought to the surface and locked back on the chambers. The pressure in the bell is maintained until it is mated with the chambers and equalized.

Once back in their pressurized living quarters, the dive teams switch out and the next team locks back into the bell, unlocks from the chamber and is lowered back to the job-site. This system enables divers to remain at depth for 20–30 days before finally decompressing.

Upon completion of the *Monitor* project, Global's saturation system became the only US Navy approved civilian saturation diving system.

ENDNOTES

1   Sea Dwellers by Bob Barth, Navy diver on all three SEALAB projects

Dave Thompson at the diving control station.

Saturation control station.

Saturation control van on Derrick Barge Wotan.

DB Wotan.

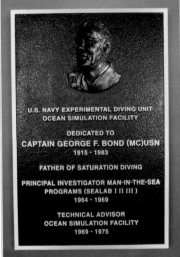

Captain George Bond, USA,
Medical Corps and
a legend in his own time.

Capt. MSC Walter Mazzone at
the control van on SEALAB III.

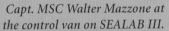

Diving bell.

Saturation diver at 240'.

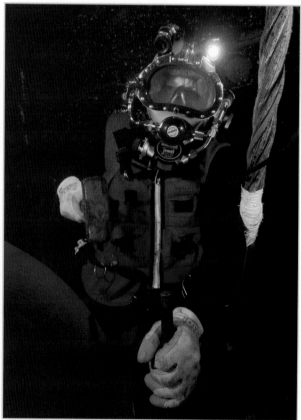

Sat diver with jewel gas-reclaim helmet.

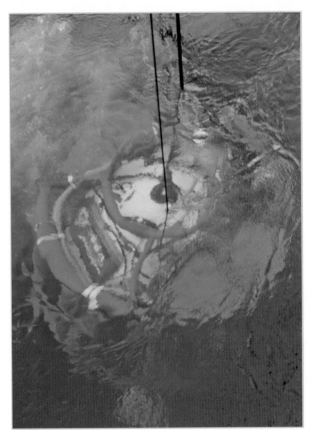

Global Diving saturation diving bell used by the US Navy on the Monitor *Project (2001).*

Accomodations in the Sat system, deck decompression chamber (DDC).

Saturation control panel.

Subs, Spooks &
U.S. Navy Divers

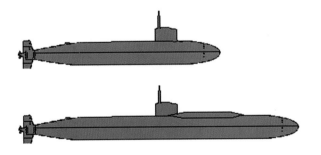

"US NAVY AQUANAUTS— DIVING THE LAST FRONTIER"

Much of the material relating to Submarine Development Group operations remains classified to this day, but with the publication of books such as *Blind Man's Bluff* [1] and the *Silent War,* [2] several interesting facts about saturation diving have come into the public domain. So, the dates and events listed below represent only those that can be gleaned from open sources without the risk of compromising national security. There has been no official confirmation or denial of this material, but more than a few shared winks and nods.

To begin to appreciate the Navy's commitment to saturation diving, it is necessary to weave together the history of not only the Navy Experimental Diving Unit (NEDU) and Deep Submergence Systems Project (DSSP), but also the activities of the specific submarines and their related Submarine Development Groups.

Early submarine disasters and the related rescue efforts drove the Navy's need to dive deeper. As a result, NEDU became the subject-matter experts on saturation diving and human performance at depth. By 1962 the Navy was involved in saturation diving with the Man-in-the-Sea project and in 1964 with Sealab 1. The same year the Deep Submergence Systems Project (DSSP) was formed. But here is where it gets interesting, when, also in 1964, DSSP becomes an asset of Naval intelligence. Why was intelligence dabbling in submarine rescue?

In 1965 Sealab II had successfully saturated divers at 205 fsw, demonstrating that they had moved passed the R&D stage and that saturation diving was now an operational capability for the Navy. The same year, Naval intelligence came up with a highly classified plan, now known as "Sand Dollar," to recover Soviet missiles and parts from the sea floor. Defense Intelligence Agency (DIA) had approved DSSP to develop deep recovery capabilities for intelligence collection — and with that came funding.

With that approval, 1965 became a very busy year for deep diving. In July the submarine USS *Halibut* was reclassified and modified for DSSP operations. A new "phantom" bathyscaphe was built in absolute secrecy by DSSP, using the Trieste as a cover. And from 1965 to 1968, twenty-eight helium-oxygen saturation dives were made at NEDU to depths of 825 feet.

But why were they modifying submarines? The Navy could not very well place a salvage ship with a saturation diving system in Soviet waters without attracting undue attention. After all, this was the Cold War period.

From 1965 to 1967, USS *Seawolf* was refueled and upgraded to the new submarine quality assurance requirements, set in place after the USS *Thresher* (SSN 593) tragedy. She also became the flagship of Submarine Squadron Two. USS *Seawolf* was cut in half to be fitted with other

DSSD diver.

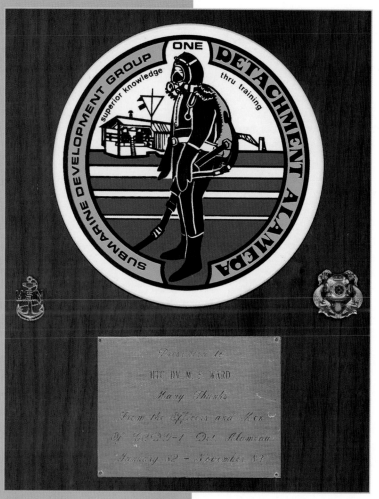

Navy diver Mike Ward's plaque
from CSDG-1 Det Alameda
(1983).

equipment and to allow for the installation of a new section that would house divers who were trained for saturation diving.

In 1967 Submarine Development Squadron FIVE was established in response to an increasing need for a single operational command to take charge and coordinate all deep submergence activities within the naval establishment. The ships and submarines attached to the command, located at Naval Submarine Base, San Diego, California, and Bangor, Washington, included deep submergence rescue vehicles and diesel and nuclear-powered research submarines, as well as surface support ships.

The USS *Scorpion* (SSN-589) went missing in May, 1968, while operating southwest of Azores — cause of accident unknown. It was later learned that *Scorpion* was not on a routine crossing of the Atlantic, but had been tasked with a top-secret mission to spy on a group of Soviet ships, including a nuclear submarine.

DSSP, under the supervision of Commander Jack Tomsky, developed the MK 2 MOD 0 Deep Diving System, and in 1968 the DDS was put aboard the *Elk River* (IX-501) to support Sealab III. The same year a record-breaking excursion dive to 1025 feet was made from a saturation depth of 825 feet at NEDU.

Also in 1968, USS *Halibut* was declared operationally ready to carry out deep intelligence gathering missions.

In 1969 Sealab III ended in disaster, but it was concluded that the Navy had "already established a group of divers who were going to interface with their equipment to two nuclear submarines and conduct intelligence operations."[3] The Navy publicly announced the project was terminated, but in reality it just went undercover.

From 1969 until 1971, USS *Halibut* underwent modification at Mare Island Ship Yard to support saturation divers. The chamber was hidden in plain sight, disguised as a DSRV attached to the rear deck of the submarine. In addition, in November, 1970, USS *Seawolf* transited the Panama Canal, changing her homeport from Groton, Connecticut to Mare Island Naval Shipyard in Vallejo, California, for conversion to a special projects platform.

In October, 1971, USS *Halibut* departed for Sea of Okhotsk to tap into Soviet communications by placing a magnetic induction unit over the cables running along the seabed, and then in August, 1972, she departed on her second collection mission. Quoting from *Blind Man's Bluff*, a temporary cable running back to the sub allowed them to listen in on Soviet military conversations for a month. The intelligence information was "pure military gold."

As the USS *Seawolf* completed her extensive post-conversion test and evaluation period in 1974, the CIA had the *Glomar Explorer* built by

Howard Hughes for the "Jennifer Project" to recover a Soviet submarine lost in 1968. The cover story was a seabed mineral mining project.

In 1975, USS *Seawolf* came under the exclusive direction of Submarine Development Group ONE, and NEDU's principal focus became saturation diving systems and procedures.

Between 1976 and 1977, USS *Seawolf's* divers, working at 400 feet, successfully tapped into Soviet communications cables in the Sea of Okhotsk, east of the Soviet Union. In 1978 USS *Parche* (SSN683) ran the same mission profile under the code name "Ivy Bells."

The Elk River supported the MK2 MOD 0 deep diving system on the SEALAB III project in 1968 and 1969.

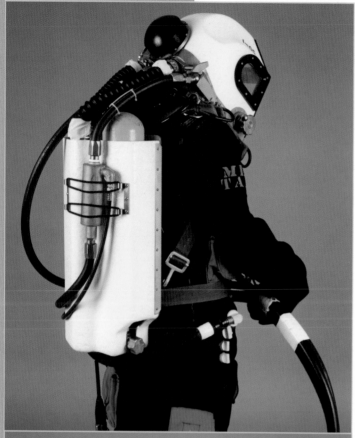

EX-14 with gas recirculator.

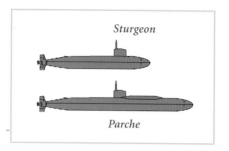

Between 1978 and 1980, USS *Parche's* divers also tapped into a cable in 500 feet of water off the Kola Peninsula, and on later missions divers would work at 600 feet in the Barents Sea, north of Russia near Murmansk. Back at NEDU, divers completed a 37-day saturation dive to 1,800 fsw in the Ocean Simulator Facility.

In the summer of 1980, USS *Parche* returned to the Okhotsk for divers to plant new taps and retrieve pods, and then to the Barents in the fall with the same mission. The collection pods, reportedly 20 feet long, 3 feet wide, and weighing 6 tons,[4] were like large tape recorders that collected the communications passing through the undersea cables which had to be periodically retrieved by the divers for download.

These highly classified operations were also becoming known to the Soviets. In November 1985 former NSA employee Ronald Pelton was arrested for espionage and selling secrets of the USS *Seawolf* and USS *Parche* to the Soviets, who had recruited him

in 1980. Authorities would also catch up with another traitor, former submariner John Walker Jr., who supplied information to the Soviets for an incredible 18 years until being turned in by his wife. Walker had been recruited in 1967.

In 1986 USS *Seawolf* conducted her last successful Western Pacific deployment and returned to Mare Island in June to prepare for decommissioning.

From 1987 to 1991, USS *Parche* was in Mare Island Shipyard for an extensive refit and to have a hundred feet added to her hull, just forward of the control room and sail, to house "research & development" equipment. The R&D function included intelligence gathering and underwater salvage. Reportedly, the *Parche* was able to support covert intelligence-gathering operations by extending a remote grapple through a hatch in the keel to salvage relatively small items from the ocean floor such as missiles, nuclear warheads, satellites, etc.

But during this same period, it was not just all about the submarines. The submarine rescue ships *Pigeon* and *Ortolan*, with their Deep Diving Systems, were still actively involved in saturation diving. In the mid-eighties, the *Elk River* was being used to train saturation divers before they disappeared "up north" to the Dev Group Detachment and to become part of a Sea Comp Team.

Then in 1989 the Soviet Union collapsed, the Cold War was over, and the much needed funding for saturation diving dried up. *Pigeon, Ortolan,* and *Elk River* were out of the saturation diving business. But *Parche* lived on.

With the modifications completed, USS *Parche* resumed Pacific Fleet operations in 1992 as part of Submarine Development Squadron FIVE, and was transferred to Naval Submarine Base Bangor, Washington, in November 1994. In 1996 Submarine Development Group ONE was

EX-14 with hot-water suit and umbilical.

re-designated Submarine Development Squadron FIVE.

SUBDEVRON 5 continues to support a Diving Systems Support Detachment (DSSD) whose stated mission is "Detachment Diving supports the evaluation of advanced diver work systems and provides training in all levels of underwater diving techniques. The detachment provides the operational base of Navy divers who have been trained in developmental underwater salvage and advanced saturation diver work systems. Det Diving also provides maintenance and diving services to Submarine Development Squadron Five units located in the PACNORWEST area."[5]

The submariners and divers, who to this day remain nameless, performed some of the most dangerous covert missions of the Cold War and were essentially unheard of until the book *Blind Man's Bluff* brought their incredible contributions to light in 1998. Some of the divers received multiple awards, such as the Legion of Merit Medal for "taking care of business" during the Cold War, but have never been given the public recognition they deserve.

Former Secretary of Defense Clifton Gates best summed it up in an address at a USS *Parche* reunion. He told a very special community of underwater US Navy personnel that their activities were key, crucial, and central to the winning of the Cold War. He could not specifically identify the participants, nor could he even hint at what they had done without compromising national security, but he wanted to tell them that they know who they are and what they had done, and that he felt that each and every one was a hero.[6]

ENDNOTES

1 *Blind Man's Bluff* by Sherry Sontag and Christopher Drew, 1998.
2 *The Silent War* by John P Craven
3 Commander Tomsky, Naval Forces Under the Sea proceedings
4 There is a photo of one of the pods in *Blind Man's Bluff.* The Soviets also have one on display in a museum in Moscow
5 Quote from SUBDEVRON 5 web page
6 Commander Tomsky, *Naval Forces Under the Sea* proceedings, 2002, US Navy, Best Publishing

DSSD diver.

The Global War
on Terrorism

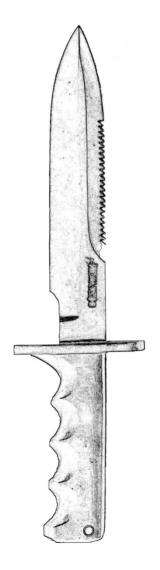

2001 – UNTIL IT'S OVER....

"No matter how long it takes, no matter where we have to look, our
United States military will patiently and surely hunt down the murderers
and killers and terrorists, and bring them, one by one, to justice."
President George W. Bush — Commander in Chief

onday, September 10, 2001 had been a crisp, clear day at
the USMC Mountain Warfare Training Center (MWTC).
It was sunset as 5th Platoon, 1st Force Recon Marines,
their faces ominously obscured under layers of green camouflage paint, went
through last minute equipment checks, preparing to be inserted into the
mountains for a five-day recon-patrol exercise. MBITR (multi-band
inter/intra-team radios) frequencies had been set and tested, sat-com
radios were safely stowed in already bulging rucksacks, PVS-17 night
sights were clamped to M-4 carbines and SAWS (squad automatic
weapons), and all loose straps were neatly taped and stowed.

Captain Fiscus and Gunny Blakey moved amongst the group
checking equipment, quietly asking questions, and giving encouragement.
It was essential that every man understood the mission and knew his
specific tasks.

The planned airborne parachute insertion had been aborted an hour
earlier when the CH-53 troop-carrying helicopters could not make the
pre-sunset time-line. With the flexibility typical of any spec-ops unit, the

*USMC Captain Fiscus, Military
Advisor, Mark Lonsdale, and
Gunny Blakey at MWTC,
September 10, 2001.*

5th platoon, Force Recon,
ready to insert.

Pre-jump preperations.

Ready for a static-line parachute jump.

platoon commander opted for a vehicle insertion to the pre-planned DZ at 7,500 feet elevation.

As the Sierra Nevadas turned purple and faded into total darkness, and before the moon could break through, the Gunny signaled the teams to saddle up and silently move out. It was impressive to see and yet not hear twenty Marines, each burdened with a hundred pounds of weapons, radios, and equipment, move off into the inky blackness without so much as a single sound.

M4 Colt carbine with M203 grenade launcher and night scope.

So by midnight I found myself with two choices. The first was to link up with the "opposition force" and try to find these phantoms—but since they had already proven themselves adept at night movement and had the advantage of Gen III night vision devices, there was little to no hope of finding them that night. So I opted for the second choice—to drive back to Los Angeles with the plan of returning to MWTC for their extract in five days.

Arriving home at five-thirty in the morning, and after two days without sleep, I showered and hit the rack. Sleep came quickly but not for long. Sometime before 0700 the phone began an incessant ringing. It was my neighbor blathering something about watching my place while I was away. "While I'm a way?" I asked groggily, "I just got home!"

Long range communications are critical to the recon mission.

She then blurted out that terrorists had attacked New York and the Pentagon and I needed to turn on the television. Flipping to CNN, I was just in time to see a passenger airliner hit the World Trade Center. Then there was footage from the Pentagon, then back to New York as the second tower was hit. Confused and half asleep, I felt like I was watching a Schwarznegger movie. Was this really the news? I quickly flipped through the local morning news line up — ABC, NBC, CBS, Fox — but all coverage was focused on New York and the Pentagon.

By mid-morning I had a passing thought about the Marine Force Recon platoon that had just disappeared into the mountains the

M249 squad automatic weapon (SAW) with collaspible para stock and PVS-17 night sight.

night before and would be emerging in five days to a very different United States. Having worked in counter-terrorism and training for over 20 years, I knew that what we were seeing was a whole new level of terrorist violence and destruction. The news media was already speculating on the potential casualties in New York, and it was in the thousands, many times more than Pearl Harbor.

But now the proverbial "gloves were coming off." The US military was going to be given the teeth to hunt and kill those who meant us harm.

AMERICA UNDER ATTACK

It was unfortunate that it took a terrorist attack of the magnitude of 9-11 for the politicians to finally take note of the threat that terrorism posed to the United States. Those in the business of international security and counter-terrorism had been beating the drum for increased security and the option of pre-emptive strikes on groups meaning us harm, but these pleas had fallen on deaf ears. The cuts to the US military and the gutting of the intelligence community during the Clinton administration had taken the United States to the level where we were defenseless against 19 angry young men, their financiers in Saudi Arabia, and their puppet masters in Afghanistan.

TWA 847

In June 1985, TWA Flight 847, coming out of Athens, was hijacked by Shi'ite terrorists, and the US Navy diving community was about to suffer its first casualty in the modern war on terrorism. A Navy diver with a Detachment of Underwater Construction Team ONE, deployed to the Naval Communication Station, Nea Makri, Greece, was on that flight.

Special operations team on a vessel boarding, search, and seizure (VBSS) mission.

Fast roping in on a maritime interdiction mission.

Because he was traveling on a military ID card and did not have a passport, this Navy diver was singled out by the terrorists, beaten, and finally executed because of his refusal to succumb to their brutality. For his bravery and "courage beyond extraordinary limits" SW2(DV) Robert Stethem was awarded the Bronze Star posthumously.

UCT 1 at NAB Little Creek commemorated one of its own with a memorial plaque, and the US Navy further honored the memory of Petty Officer Stethem by naming an Arliegh Burke Class Destroyer, DDG-63, the USS *Stethem*.

USS *COLE* — OPERATION DETERMINED RESPONSE

Thursday, October 12, 2000: Secretary of Defense William S. Cohen announces, "At 5:15 this morning, Washington time, a large explosion blew a hole in the hull of the USS *Cole* as she was mooring at Aden, Yemen, to refuel. According to current reports, five sailors are dead, 36 are wounded, and 12 are still missing. These numbers are likely to change as we learn more."

Numerous US Navy diving assets were immediately dispatched to the scene as part of what was to become OPERATION DETERMINED RESPONSE.

While refueling in the port of Aden, terrorists in a small boat packed with explosives pulled alongside the guided-missile destroyer USS *Cole* (DDG 67) and detonated a massive charge that ripped a 40-foot hole in the hull. The damage to the ship was devastating, port and forward bulkheads were blown inward, 17 sailors were killed, and 39 wounded.

EOD divers involved in demining operations in Yemen were the first to respond, immediately initiating a search for additional explosive devices. They were soon augmented by additional EOD divers out of Bahrain.

After completing a thorough hull search, the divers conducted an initial damage survey for the Navy salvage engineers working on stability calculations. It was also obvious that penetration into the torn hull would be necessary to search for the missing crewmembers.

Divers from MDSU-2 DET Alpha, deployed aboard the ocean tug USNS *Mohawk* (T-ATF-170) near Bari, Italy, were ordered to the scene. Using surface-supplied gear, the divers were tasked with locating the missing sailors, assisting with stabilizing the ship, recovery of evidence, and making structural inspections.

The first MDSU2 divers to board the *Cole* were CWO3 Frank Perna (the OIC of DET Alpha), ENCS (MDV) Lyle Becker, and BMC (DV) David Hunter. They found the ship to be blackened by the explosion, listing slightly to port, and without electrical power. Their first objectives were to determine which locations to search, identify a centralized location to setup the dive station, and determine how to safely enter the flooded spaces.[1]

By this time, close to 100 investigators, diving and salvage experts, engineers, and support teams formed the Crisis Response Team that the Navy had assembled for the grim task. This included CDR Keenan, Officer in Charge of Ship Repair Unit, Bahrain, who would head all of the salvage operations surrounding the *Cole*, LCDR Long, CDR Bobbie Scholley, CO MDSU 2, senior engineers from SIMA, and Norfolk Naval Shipyard workers.

*SW 2 (DV) Robert Stethem being
dressed-in.*

Stethem with the MK 12.

MDSU divers would use a Light Weight Dive System (LWDS), MK 21 helmets, a Divers Underwater Camera Television System (DUCTS), and Divers Helmet Mounted Lighting Systems (DHMLS). An Emergency Gas Supply (EGS) with a 150-foot whip was used instead of man-carried bailout bottles to reduce the diver's profile in the water as they moved through the tight spaces and engineering compartments.

Working in near-zero visibility and extreme heat, negotiating significant amounts debris and wreckage, the divers successfully recovered all of the missing sailors. Throughout, dive supervisors had to monitor the divers' fatigue and hydration levels very closely, since air temperatures hit 100–110 degrees, water was around 90 degrees, and the divers wore wetsuits for protection. The dive team was also able to assist the FBI by searching compartments that their agents had deemed too dangerous to enter.

In addition to CWO3 Frank Perna, ENCS (MDV) Lyle Becker, and BMC (DV) David Hunter, the other divers that participated in the hazardous operations included HT2 (DV) Bret Husbeck, EN2 (DV) Mike Shields, ETC (DV) Terry Breaux, IS3 (DV) Greg Sutherland, HMC (DV) Don Adams, GM3 (DV) Sean Baker, BM2 (DV) Mike Allison, GM2 (DV) Roger Ziliak, and STG2 (SW/DV) Schappert.

Through all this, the *Cole*'s crew had worked tirelessly under dangerous and arduous conditions to try and stabilize the crippled ship. EOD divers, SEALs, and Marines had also contributed significantly to the effort.

When the recovery phase was completed, the dive team began the inspection dives needed to determine how much of the *Cole*'s structural strength had been lost. They then assisted the move of the *Cole* to the ship that would transport her back to the United States for repair.

USS Cole.

THE PENTAGON IS ATTACKED

At approximately 09:45 on 11 SEPT 2001, the Pentagon came under attack by radical fundamentalists. After taking control of American Airlines Flight 77, a 757 loaded with innocent souls, hijackers intentionally piloted the aircraft into the side of the Pentagon, killing 125 (including Captain Bob Dolan, an ex-Navy diver), in the building, all 59 aboard the plane, and injuring 110 others.

The plane had hit at ground level, but thankfully, this section of the Pentagon had just been renovated and was not fully occupied. In addition, the floors above, 3rd, 4th, and 5th floors, stayed up for another 45 minutes, allowing more people to escape or be rescued. The armored windows and fire protection that had been installed during the renovation of that section also mitigated some of the damage. Plus the inside walls on the outer ring are lined with a kevlar material (the material used in body armor) to prevent shrapnel from entering the occupied space. Had the hijacked plane hit an area that had not been renovated, or was fully occupied, the disaster could have been quantifiably worse.

As a testament to the strength and resolve of the American people, the damage to the Pentagon was repaired in record time. The construction workers working on Project Phoenix considered it an honor to be part of the effort to bring the US military command structure back to full capability. And right there in the rubble, working on the renovation, was former First Class Diver SW2 (DV) Patrick Stethem, the brother of SW2 (DV) Robert Stethem, who had been killed by terrorists in 1985. Like his brother, Patrick had served two tours with UCT-1 in Little Creek and, after 9-11, went on to continue serving with pride as a civilian contractor on the Pentagon project.

Pentagon damage post-9/11.

But not to dwell on the tragedy, the US military response was swift, deadly, and effective. Although the Pentagon had been damaged, it in no way hindered the national command authority (NCA) from identifying the attackers and going after their leaders, cohorts, and bases in Afghanistan — al Qaeda.

OPERATION ENDURING FREEDOM

Through September and October, 2001, in conjunction with other branches of the services, Navy assets were moved into the Arabian Sea south of Afghanistan. By 07 OCT 2001, the US military had approximately 33,000 personnel in theatre when the air campaign began. Working from their carrier groups, Navy and Marine Corps pilots, along with their land-based Air Force brethren, began a precision bombing campaign of all identifiable enemy camps, material, and targets of opportunity.

To support ground operations, on 13 October the USS *Kitty Hawk* was deployed in theatre to serve as a "lily pad" for special operations forces. This carrier would serve as an Afloat Forward-Staging Base (AFSB) that would position special operations assets within easy striking distance of their targets, but still keep them safe from terrorist attack.

In support of the air campaign, US special operations forces, including Navy SEALs, were inserted into Afghanistan to seek out and mark targets for destruction. By getting "eyes on the target," special operations personnel were able to vector in attack aircraft armed with precision-guided munitions by "painting" the targets with laser target designators or relaying GPS coordinates for terminal guidance of J-DAMs (GPS-guided bombs).

Concurrent to the air and ground campaigns, a full range of US Navy ships and diving assets were deployed to support maritime interdiction operations and fleet security. In the Arabian Sea, Navy SEALs and SOC Marines were boarding ships, preventing the smuggling of terrorists, weapons, and explosives in and out of the theatre of operations. Mine counter-measures had also become a concern for shipping in the waters adjacent to military operations.

In November, 2001, preceded by SEALs and Recon Marines, Battalion Landing Team 1/1, 15th MEU (SOC), landed in Southern Afghanistan at what was to become known as Camp Rhino. This was the furthest inland that a Marine BLT had deployed, some 400 miles from their support ships. This combat deployment opened a new chapter in Marine Corps war fighting that required significant air support from US Navy and Marine helicopter pilots and logisticians.

Even though Afghanistan is land-locked, eliminating any combat swimming or diving missions for the Recon Marines, they were not going to be left out of the fray. By December, Force Recon and Light Armored Reconnaissance (LAR) teams were pushing 100 kilometers north of Rhino in their heavily armed vehicles to interdict al Qaeda and Taliban terrorist militias moving on Route 1 from Kandahar to Lashkar Gar.

Also not deterred by the lack of water, in January and February, 2002, SEALs, as part of Task Force K-Bar, were combing the caves around Zhawar Kili and the Jaji Mountains of eastern Afghanistan on Sensitive Site Exploitation (SSE) missions. SEALs were successful not only in killing numerous terrorists but also in locating massive amounts of weapons, ordnance, ammunition, and high value intelligence information. Supported by Navy EOD, they were also successful in destroying huge

MDSU2 divers on the USS Cole.

Patrick Stethem (right).

stockpiles of al Qaeda and Taliban war fighting material, along with enemy cave complexes and support infrastructure.

OPERATION IRAQI FREEDOM

The US Navy and Marine Corps' participation in Operation Iraqi Freedom was not unlike their experience in Afghanistan. The key difference was that CENTCOM opted to send in the ground forces ahead of the air campaign, which totally threw the Iraqi military off balance, resulting in desertions of Iraqi soldiers en masse. So much for the most feared army in the Middle East—just like their terrorist cohorts, they cut and ran when faced by real warfighters. And no surprise, their mighty leader was found cowering in a hole like a scared rat.

However, as SEALs combed the deserts looking for Iraqi special forces and fedayeen, and Marines led the way into Baghdad, their web-footed brothers-in-arms were again running diving operations in the south. SEALs, Recon Marines, EOD divers, and Navy divers, all part of Naval Special Clearance Team ONE (NSCT-1), were instrumental in locating and destroying numerous mines and hazards in the northern Arabian Gulf and on the approach into the port city of Umm Qasr.

Working under the multi-national Combined Task Unit 55.4.3, NSCT divers worked alongside UK Fleet Diving Unit Three, Australia's Clearance Dive Team, and EOD Mobile Units Six and Eight. NSCT also successfully deployed UUV assets and marine mammals as they continued to develop new tactics and techniques for future mine hunting operations.

Navy SEALs interview villagers in the mountains of Afghanistan.

THE ON-GOING WAR ON TERRORISM

As this book goes to print, the United States is fully engaged in the war on terrorism. The gloves did come off in 2001, and the full lethality of the US military has been thrown against the enemies of the free world. But more importantly, these recent operations have given our commanders and planners the opportunity to re-evaluate how we go to war and how we fight terrorism.

In addition to the all-important "lessons learned" that have been collected on the tactical level, strategic thinking is also being re-worked. The Navy's Deep Blue operations group is studying the concept of Afloat Forward Staging Bases (AFSB) for future operations and researching ways to better integrate special operations forces into naval warfare.

SEALs will continue to dominate the littoral zone, but as the ultimate quick reaction force, the Marines are rethinking their prior operational limitation to coastal regions. Future warfare will see Marines projecting their combat capabilities several hundred miles inland, forcing their naval combat support assets to come up with ways and means to better support these operations.

Considering the magnitude of the task, the global war on terrorism will continue into the next decade, and Navy divers will continue to be an integral part of that effort. Where the SEALs and Naval aviators may enjoy some level of

SEALS clearing caves during sensitive site exploitation (SSE) missions.

SEALs inspect an Al Qaeda-Taliban ammunition cache, winter of 2001/2002.

SEAL fast attack vehicle (FAV).

glamour in their missions, Navy divers will continue to handle the tough, ugly jobs in dark waters.

Force protection is becoming ever more important, as terrorists have already demonstrated their willingness to attack both US military and civilian shipping. It is a big ocean out there, making it all but impossible to stop one terrorist with a satchel charge or a rubber boat loaded with explosives. The responsibility for surface force protection against these threats falls to the sailors and Marines on deck watch, but below the surface, Navy divers will continue to be called upon to sweep for mines, inspect port facilities, and repair the damage when one angry man slips through the net.

> "We will not tire, we will not falter, and we will not fail."
> President George W. Bush – Commander in Chief

ENDNOTES

1   OPERATION DETERMINED RESPONSE By: CWO3 Frank Perna. MDSU 2 Det Alpha Lends a Hand to A Wounded Warrior

Fast roping onto the deck of a moving ship.

*SEAL sniper covers ship boarding
training operation.*

*SEALs execute a sensitive site
exploration (SSE) mission in
Zhawar Kili region (2002).*

Into the Future

As NASA continues to probe the reaches of outer space and place ROVs on Mars, the engineers at Coastal Systems Station (CSS) will continue to develop new technology to make the underwater world more accessible. Millions, if not billions, of dollars will be spent on developing state-of-the-art deep-diving ROVs, submarine rescue systems, mine reconnaissance UUVs, and automated mine recovery equipment. But none of this technology will ever replace the humble MK1 Mod 0 Navy Diver.

As long as ships sail across oceans and aircraft fly over water, disasters at sea will occur, and salvage divers will continue to be called upon to locate and recover the wreckage. Similarly, just as the Navy will always need husbandry divers to service the fleet, change screws, and weld up damaged hulls, construction divers will be needed to build and maintain the port facilities, drive piles, repair docks, and lay cable across the sea floor. The future work for EOD divers and SEALs is self-evident with the current war on terrorism.

To meet the demand for these highly trained and motivated individuals, the Navy Dive School is assured its rightful place in both the history and future of the United States NAVY. Naval Diving & Salvage Training Center will continue to be the hub of this important wheel, educating and training young men and women to go where the rubber meets the road, or in this case, the wetsuit meets the water.

Then there are the Master Divers — the very embodiment of NAVY Diving. Steeped in tradition, fueled by rum, cured in salt and baked in the sun, the tattooed and barrel-chested Master Diver is out there in the fleet bringing his own brand of motivation to the up-and-coming deep-sea divers. Dispensing threats of bodily harm, tempered with sage advice, it is the Master Divers who are entrusted as the gatekeepers. They control the gates to Neptune's dark realm, where only the best and the bravest are privileged to work.

Finally, to the next generation of Navy Divers who have heard spine-chilling tales of just how tough military diving can be: It is! Don't for one second think that future technology will make the diver's job easier or warmer. The life of

T-shirt designs of the Navy diving community.

a working military diver is both physically demanding and highly rewarding. Demanding because it is cold, dirty work in often horrendous conditions, but rewarding because the Navy Deep Sea Diver, EOD Diver, SEAL, or Recon Marine does a job that only few can imagine, and even fewer would attempt.

HOO YAH Navy Divers!!

Master Diver reunion, 2003.

Appendix A

SPONSORS SECTION

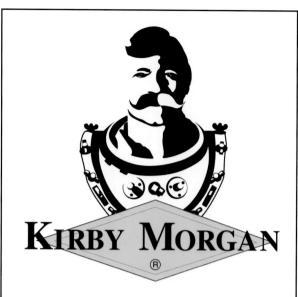

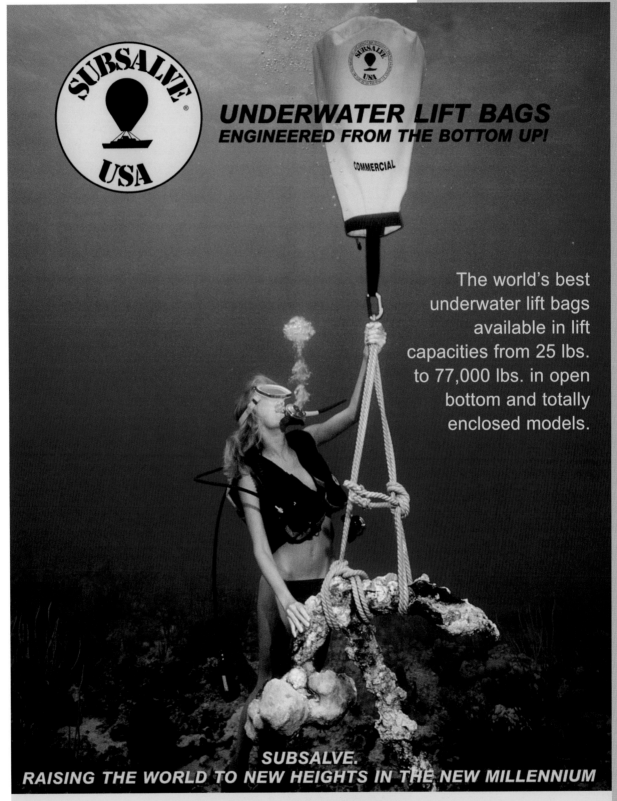

  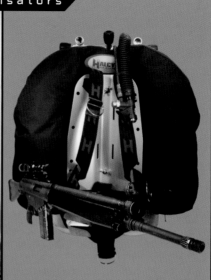

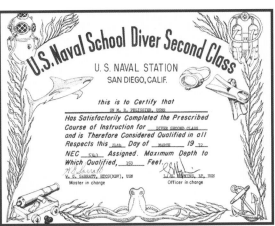

Appendix B

ABBREVIATIONS

ADS	Atmospheric Diving Suit (ADS 2000)
ADDS	Advanced Deep Diving System
AGE	Arterial Gas Embolism
ANU	Authorized for Navy Use
ARG	Amphibious Ready Group
ASDS	Advanced Seal Delivery System (Seal's new dry sub)
ARS	Auxiliary Rescue Salvage vessel
ASW	Anti-Submarine Warfare
BDO	Basic Diving Officer
BLT	Battalion Landing Team
BM	Boatswain's Mate
BT	Bottom Time
BUD/S	Basic Underwater Demolition / Seal school
CAX	Cheatham Annex (ESSM warehouse Williamsburg, VA)
CB	Construction Battalion (Seabees)
CCBA	Closed Circuit Breathing Apparatus
CDR	Commander
CDU	Consolidated Divers Unit
CDU	Combat Demolition Unit (WWII)
CMC	Command Master Chief
CNET	Chief of Naval Education & Training
CINC	Commander in Chief
CIV	Civilian
CJTF	Combined Joint Task Force
CO	Commanding Officer
COMCAM	Combat Camera
CONUS	Continental United States
COTS	Commercial Off-the-Shelf (something the Pentagon needs more of)
CPO	Chief Petty Officer (E-7)
CS	Senior Chief
CSS	Coastal Systems Station
CWO	Chief Warrant Officer
DC	Damage Control
DCIEM	Defence and Civil Institute of Environmental Medicine, Canada
DCS	Decompression Sickness
DDC	Deck Decompression Chamber
DDS	Deep Diving System

DDS Mk-1	Transportable Deep Diving System
DDS Mk-2	Ship-board Deep Diving System
DDS	Dry Deck Shelter for SDV
DET	Detachment
DEVGROUP	Development Group (Seal Team 6)
DFC	Diver First Class
DHMLS	Divers Helmet Mounted Lighting System
DIA	Defense Intelligence Agency
DLSS	Diver Life Support Systems
DMO	Diving Medical Officer
DMT	Diving Medical Technician
DO	Diving Officer
DO	Duty Officer
DOD	Department of Defense
DPV	Diver Propulsion Vehicle
DSC	Diver Second Class
DSI	Diving Systems International
DSRV	Deep Submergence Rescue Vehicle
DSSP	Deep Submergence Systems Development
DSU	Deep Submergence Unit
DUCTS	Divers Underwater Camera Television System
E	Enlisted (example E-7 Chief Petty Officer)
ED	Engineering Duty Officer
EDF	Experimental Diving Facility
EDO	Engineering Duty Officer
EDU	Experimental Diving Unit
EGS	Emergency Gas System (Come-home or bail-out bottle)
EL	Entry Lock used to mate PTC to DDC
EMT	Emergency Medical Technician
END	Equivalent Narcosis Depth
EOD	Explosive Ordnance Disposal
EODMU	EOD Mobile Unit
EPs	Emergency Procedures
ESSM	Emergency Ship Salvage Material
FADL	Fly Away Dive Locker
FADS	Fly Away Diving System
FARCC	Fly Away Recompression Chamber
FCCA	Fleet Combat Camera Atlantic
FFM	Full Face Mask
FFW	Feet of Fresh Water
FMGS	Fly Away Mixed Gas System (FADS III)
FSW	Feet of Sea Water
G250	Scubapro regulator
HCU	Harbor Clearance Unit
He	Helium
HeliOx	Deep diving mixture of helium and oxygen
HEO2	Helium / Oxygen mixture
HM	Hospital Corpsman
HT	Hull Technician
IDV	Integrated Diver's Vest
INSS	Integrated Navigational Sonar System
JCCC	Joint Combat Camera Center (DC)
JCS	Joint Chiefs of Staff
J-SOC	Joint Special Operations Command
JTF	Joint Task Force
KMB	Kirby-Morgan Bandmask
LAR-V	Draeger rebreather (Mk-25)
LAR-VII	O_2 / Nitrox rebreather
LCD	Liquid Crystal Display
LCDR	Lieutenant Commander
LDS	Lightweight Diving System
LMRS	Long-term Mine Reconnaissance System
LPO	Lead Petty Officer
LSS	Life Support Skid
LT	Lieutenant
LWDS	Lightweight Diving System

MCC	Main Control Console
MCD	Marine Corps Diver
MCM	Mine Counter Measures
MDSU	Marine Diving & Salvage Unit
MDV	Master Diver
MEU	Marine Expeditionary Unit
Mk-1 Mod 0	Lightweight Bandmask (KMB)
Mk-3	Lightweight Fly Away Diving System (MK III)
Mk-5	Old Heavy Gear with brass and copper helmet (MK V)
Mk-8 Boat	Seal delivery wet sub (SDV)
Mk-9 Boat	Smaller version of the SDV
Mk-10	Closed-circuit mixed gas diving system designed to be used for PTC lock-outs to 1500 fsw
Mk-11	Semi-closed circuit mixed-gas system consisting of a helmet and re-circulating backpack designed for use to 850 fsw
Mk-12	Navy air diving helmet
Mk-14	Semi-closed mixed gas system with Mk 12 type helmet
Mk-15	Mixed gas rebreather
Mk-16	Non-magnetic mixed gas rebreather used by EOD and SDV drivers
Mk-20	Aga lightweight full-face mask
Mk-21	Navy version of the Superlite 17 diving helmet
Mk-22 Mod 0	Navy version of the DSI-18B Bandmask
Mk-24	Aga full-face mask used with Mk 16 rebreather
Mk-25	Draeger closed-circuit oxygen rebreather (LAR-V) used by Seals and USMC Recon combatant swimmers
M 48	Latest DSI full-face mask
MM	Machinist's Mate
MOD	Model
MSF	Mobile Support Facility
NAVFAC	Naval Facilities
NAVSEA	Naval Sea Systems Command
NAVSTA	Naval Station
NCA	National Command Authority
NCDU	Naval Combat Demolitions Unit (WWII)
NDSTC	Naval Diving & Salvage Training Center
NEC	Naval Educational Code
NEDU	Naval Experimental Diving Unit
NMRI	Naval Medical Research Institute
NSDS	Navy Diving School (Salvage) (circa 1942)
NSSC	Naval Sea Systems Command
NSW	Naval Special Warfare
NSWG	Naval Special Warfare Group
NUWC	Naval Undersea Warfare Center
OEF	Operation Enduring Freedom
OIC	Officer in Charge
OIF	Operation Iraqi Freedom
OOC	Double O Charlie Commander of Diving & Salvage
OPs	Operational Procedures
OSF	Ocean Simulation Facility (at NEDU)
OTS	Ocean Technology Systems U/W communications
O2	Oxygen
PAC	Pacific
PAO	Public Affairs Officer
PIO	Public Information Officer
POC	Point of Contact
PPO2	Partial Pressure of Oxygen
PQS-2A	Underwater sonar for mine detection
PRMA	Personnel Rescue Module System for sub rescue
PT	Physical Training
PTC	Personnel Transfer Capsule / Diving Bell
PVA	Pressure Vessel Assembly
RM	Royal Marine
ROV	Remote Operated Vehicle
SAS	Special Air Service (British, Australian & New Zealand)
SAT	Saturation Diving

SBU	Special Boat Unit
SBS	Special Boat Service (Royal Marine Commandos)
SCUBA	Self Contained Underwater Breathing Apparatus
SDS	Saturation Diving System
SDV	SEAL or Swimmer Delivery Vehicle
SDVT	SDV Team
SEAL	Sea, Air & Land
SECDEF	Secretary of Defense
SELRES	Select Reserve
SF	Special Forces
SFUO	Special Forces Underwater Operations
SIMA	Shore Intermediate Maintenance Activity
SL-17	DSI SuperLite diving helmet similar to Mk-21
SOF	Special Operations Force
SOCOM	Special Operations Command
SOP	Standard Operating Procedure
SPECWAR	Special Warfare
SPG	Submersible Pressure Gauge
SRC	Submarine Rescue Chamber
SRT	Special Response Team
SSDS	Surface-Supplied Diving System
ST	Seal Team
STT	Seal Tactical Training
SUBDEVRON	Submarine Development Squadron
SUPSALV	Supervisor of Salvage & Diving
SWCC	Special Warfare Combatant Crewman
TM	Team
UBA	Underwater Breathing Apparatus
UCT	Underwater Construction Team / Seabees
UDM	Underwater Depth Monitors
UDT	Underwater Demolition Team
UHMS	Undersea and Hyperbaric Medical Society
UMO	Undersea Medical Officer
USA	United States Army
USD	United States Divers (now Aqualung)
USMC	United States Marine Corps
USN	United States Navy
UUV	Unmanned Undersea Vehicle
U/W	Underwater
UWSH	Underwater Ship Husbandry
UXB	Un-Exploded Bomb
WARCOM	Special Warfare Command
VSW	Very Shallow Water (mine counter measures)
XO	Executive Officer
YDT	Yard Diving Tender vessel
00C	Double O Charlie – SUPSALV Supervisor of Salvage & Diving
00C3	Supervisor of Diving
1C	One Charlie – First Class Diver
2C	Two Charlie – Second Class Diver

Appendix C

RECOMMENDED ADDITIONAL READING

NAVAL FORCES UNDER THE SEA—Best Publishing

US NAVY DIVING MANUAL—Revision 5—Best Publishing

THE TERRIBLE HOURS by Peter Maas

DESCENT INTO DARKNESS by Commander Edward C. Raymer

BLIND MAN'S BLUFF by Sherri Sontag & Christopher Drew

THE SILENT WAR by John P Craven

BRAVE MEN—DARK WATERS by Orr Kelly

ONE PERFECT OP by Command Master Chief Dennis Chalker, USN (Ret.)

SEA DWELLERS by Bob Barth

PAPA TOPSIDE edited by Helen Siiteri—Naval Institute Press

UNDERWATER WARRIORS by Paul Kemp

HELMETS OF THE DEEP by Leon Lyons

NOAA MANUAL—Best Publishing

1905 MANUAL FOR DIVERS Handbook For Seaman Gunners

SRT DIVER by Mark V. Lonsdale

BEST PUBLISHING—www.bestpub.com